I8

FRANCE LIVE

Danièle Bourdais
Sue Finnie

OXFORD
UNIVERSITY PRESS

OXFORD
UNIVERSITY PRESS

Great Clarendon Street, Oxford OX2 6DP

Oxford University Press is a department of the University of Oxford.
It furthers the University's objective of excellence in research,
scholarship, and education by publishing worldwide in

Oxford New York

Auckland Bangkok Buenos Aires Cape Town Chennai
Dar es Salaam Delhi Hong Kong Istanbul Karachi Kolkata
Kuala Lumpur Madrid Melbourne Mexico City Mumbai
Nairobi São Paulo Shanghai Taipei Tokyo Toronto

Oxford is a registered trade mark of Oxford University Press
in the UK and in certain other countries

British Library Cataloguing in Publication Data

Data available

ISBN 0 19 912398 5

10 9 8 7 6 5 4 3 2 1

Printed in Italy by G. Canale & C. SpA

Acknowledgements

*The publishers would like to thank the following for their permission to
reproduce photographs:*

Cover: Dick Capel-Davies, Corel Professional Photos, Getty
Images/Fremont, Le Monde website, PhotoAlto

Title page: Getty Images/Fremont

p5: Photothèque Wallis/Moura (top left), Corel Professional
Photos (top right), Photothèque Wallis/Souret (centre),
Photothèque Wallis/Garufi (bottom left and right); **p6**: IMSI's
Masterclips Collection (top left), Empics (top right and centre),
Hemera Technologies (bottom left); **p7**: Corbis/Yves Forestier
Symga; **p8**: Photothèque Wallis/Garufi (left), Tony Lees (right);
p9: OUP (top right and bottom), Getty/Image Bank (left);
p10: Photothèque Wallis/Mauregard; **p11**: Corbis; **p12**: Das
Photos; **p13**: OUP (left), Photothèque Wallis/Detienda (right);
p14: Photothèque Wallis/Labbe, Photothèque Wallis/Leyreloup;
p15: Objectif Photos; **p16**: Objectif photos (inset), Corbis/Owen
Franken; **p17**: Das Photos (top), Hemera Technologies (bottom);
p18: Getty Images/Fremond (top), Corbis (bottom); **p20**: Das
photos; **p21**: Photothèque Wallis/Royer; **p22**: Empics (top and
bottom left), Photothèque Wallis/Fichaux (bottom right);
p23: Empics (top), Das photos (centre), Phototheque
Wallis/Poulet-Mission (bottom); **p24**: OUP (top), Das photos
(bottom); **p25**: OUP; **p26**: Photothèque Wallis/Duranti;
p27: Hemera Technologies (all); **p28**: Keith Gibson (top),
Photothèque Wallis/Giani (bottom left), Corbis (bottom right);
p29: Keith Gibson; **p30**: AA World Travel Agency (top);
Corbis/Marc Garanger (bottom); **p31**: Corbis/Charles & Josette
Lenars (top); Photothèque Wallis/C.Moirenc (bottom); **p32**: Das
photos; **p33**: Photothèque Wallis/Duchene (top left), Photothèque
Wallis/Demeurs (top right), Photothèque Wallis/Gouron (bottom
left), D Capel-Davies (bottom right); **p34**: Photothèque
Wallis/C.Moirenc; **p35**: Das photos; **p36**: Corbis/Reuters New
Media Inc; **p37**: OUP (left), AFP/Dominique Faget-STF (right);
p38: OUP; **p39**: Corbis/Sygma Hekimian Julian (top); Empics
(bottom); **p40**: Photothèque Wallis/G.Martin-Reget, Photothèque
Wallis/Gouron, Photothèque Wallis/Leyreloup (bottom); **p41**: Das
Photos (top), Photothèque Wallis/Blache-Mission (2nd top),
Objectif Photos (3rd top), Photothèque Wallis/Clea (left), Objectif
Photos (right), Photothèque Wallis/Garufi (inset); **p42**: Das
Photos; **p43**: Corbis (top), Getty Images (bottom);
p44: Photothèque Wallis/Duranti (top), Das Photos (centre), Corel
Professional Photos (bottom); **p45**: R Roberts; **p46**: Corbis;
p47: Corbis/Reuters New Media Inc (top left), Corbis, Franz-Marc
Frei (top right), Corel Professional Photos (bottom left),
Corbis/Ray Juno (bottom right); **p48**: Corel Professional photos;
p49: AFP/Edition Poupard (left), Photothèque Wallis/Duranti
(right); **p50**: Corbis/Nick Wheeler; **p51**: Corbis/AFP (top),
Corbis/Robert Holmes (bottom); **p52**: Corbis/AFP (top), Seafrance
(bottom); **p53**: Rex Features; **p54**: Stone (top), Corbis/Owen
Franken (bottom); **p55**: Archivo Iconografico S.A./Corbis/RM (top),
D Capel-Davies (bottom); **p56**: Bridgeman/Giraudon (top), Mary
Evans (2nd top and bottom), Hulton Archive (3rd top),
Corbis/Gianni Dagli Orti (4th top); **p57**: Bridgeman/Giraudon
(top), Corbis/Bettmann (right), Das Photos (left); **p59**: Rex/Sipa;
p60: Corbis/Sygma Langevin Jaques (top left), Corbis/sygma
Romane P. (bottom left), Rex/Sipa (right); **p61**: Corbis/Sygma
Pavlovsky Jacques; **p62**: AA World Travel Library (top),
Corbis/Peter Turnley (bottom); **p65**: AFP/Jacques Demarthon-STP
(left), OUP (right); **p66**: Corbis/Chris Bland (right), Semaine de la
Presse (left); **p67**: Corbis/Edward Holub; **p68**: Corbis/Tim
Thompson (top), Das Photos (bottom); **p69**: Getty Images;
p70: Corbis/Thomas Jouanneau/Symga (left),
Corbis/L'Humanité/Keystone/Sygma (right); **p72**: Corbis/Pitchal
Frederick/Sygma (top), R Roberts (bottom); **p73**: Corbis/Tom
Stewart (right), Corbis/Reuters New Media Inc (left);
p74: Corbis/AFP (top), Corbis/Frances Stephane/Symga (bottom);
p75: Corbis/Attar Maher/Sygma

Illustrations are by: Stefan Chabluk (maps and charts) and
Frédérique Vayssieres (cartoons).

Introduction

France Live is a culture book for school-aged students of French. It comprises 18 chapters covering a range of relevant and interesting topics.

France Live will help meet the aims of the QCA scheme of work and the Cultural knowledge and Contact strand of the Modern Languages Framework. It can be used alongside any course book, and the differentiated material makes it ideal for students working at different levels.

There are also linked KS3 and KS4 worksheets for every chapter of the book on our subscription site, **www.oup.com/uk/i-café**. These contain articles in French with associated activities and support material.

Contents

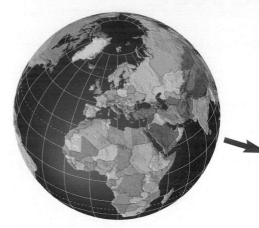

▲ A spot-on location

Situated half way between the Equator and the North Pole, France has a temperate climate and rich soil. A lucky position to be in!

▲ Space and good neighbours

France is the largest country in Europe after Russia and lies at the western tip of the continent. It is a country with a view, as it is bordered by three seas (the Channel, the Atlantic Ocean and the Mediterranean Sea). Yet it is never far from the action as it has eight neighbours (Belgium, Luxembourg, Germany, Switzerland, Italy, Monaco, Andorra and Spain) and is only 35 kms away from the south coast of Britain, to which it has been linked by the Eurotunnel since 1994.

- **Surface area:** 550 000 square km
  (UK: 244 000 square km)

- **North to South:** 1 000 km
  (UK: 960 km)

- **West to East:** 945 km
  (UK: 480 km)

- **Highest mountain:**
  Mont Blanc: 4 897 m
  (UK: Ben Nevis, 1 343 m)

- **Longest river:** Loire: 1 012 km
  (UK: Severn, 354 km)

► Great looks and a nickname

France has varied landscapes: 5 500 km of coastline, ancient mountains ranges in the centre, high snow-covered peaks in the south, low flat lands in the north, rolling green countryside along the Loire. 25% of the land is covered in forests and there are 150 lakes.

France is often known as *l'Hexagone*, because of its six-sided shape.

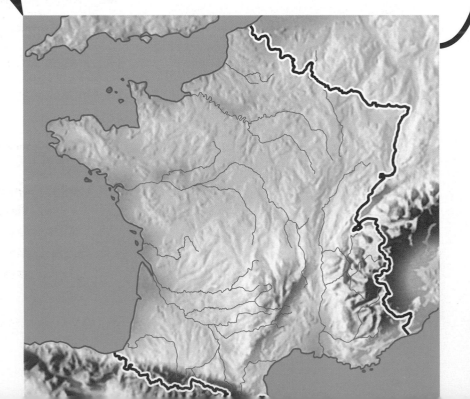

◀ A nice crowd

The population of France is the second largest in the European Union, after Germany. It holds the record for life expectancy. 83 years for women (75.5 for men).

France's population is also one of the most multicultural in Europe: one in four families has a parent or grandparent who wasn't born in France. Great for choice of food and music!

▼ Places to see and be seen!

Almost 80% of French people live in small or medium-sized towns. There are not many really large cities. The largest is the capital, Paris: it has a central influence over the rest of the country and is a symbol of French culture in the world. But France isn't just Paris!

- **Population:** 61.1 million
  (UK: 59.7 million)

- **Density:** 107 inhabitants per square km (UK: 241)

- **Capital (Paris)** – Paris and suburbs: 10.9 million (London: 7 million)

- **Other main cities:** Lyon (1.6 m), Marseille-Aix-en-Provence (1.4 m) (Greater Manchester: 2.5 million and Birmingham: 1 million)

Bonjour! Je m'appelle Lucas Martin. J'ai 13 ans. Je suis français. J'habite près de Toulouse, dans le sud-ouest. Ici, c'est super!

Salut! Moi, c'est Malika Derrouaz. J'ai 13 ans. Je suis française. Mes grands-parents sont algériens. J'habite à Paris. Bienvenue en France!

1 Read the information on pages 4 and 5 and do the quiz. Explain your answers.

 a Is France's geographical location a good one?

 b What is on each of the sides of the *Hexagone*?

 c Why are there more French women than French men?

 d What is special about 25% of the French?

2 Using a dictionary, list the names of the countries and seas surrounding France, in French. Then do the same for Britain.

3 Choose a topic and write a short paragraph in English.

 a Highlight the similarities and differences between France and Britain based on the information here.

 b Should the capital city lead the country as Paris tends to do? Make a case for or against.

 c Do you think it is a good thing for France to have a multicultural society? Why?

French history is rich in events that have shaped the country and given it its national symbols.

The oldest symbol is the *coq gaulois* or Gallic rooster, a reminder of when France was called Gaul: the Latin word *gallus* meant both Gaul and rooster. It is the emblem of French sports teams in international competitions and features in the logo of a world famous French brand of sportswear: *Le Coq Sportif*.

The *Tricolore* flag was born during the French Revolution, in 1794, combining the colours of Paris (red and blue) and that of the king (white). It flies above public buildings together with the European flag, at most civil and military ceremonies and decorates the faces of football supporters!

France is a Republic as indicated by the letters *RF (République française)* on French euro coins. The Franc was the currency of France until it was replaced by the euro (€) in January 2002.

The most prominent symbol of France is the figure of a woman, Marianne, whose origins are unclear. Her statue, found in town halls and law courts, has recently been modeled on famous actresses, e.g. Brigitte Bardot, Catherine Deneuve and Laetitia Casta.

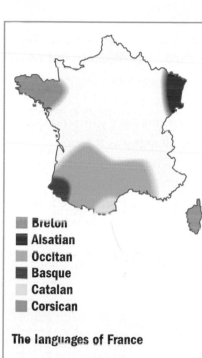

■ **Breton**
■ **Alsatian**
■ **Occitan**
■ **Basque**
■ **Catalan**
■ **Corsican**

The languages of France

Official language: French

Regional languages: Breton, Corsican, Occitan, Basque, Catalan, Alsatian (taught in some schools up to University level in an effort to keep them alive)

French-speaking world

There are now 160 million speakers of French in the world (including France and the French overseas territories)

(460 million speakers of English)

July 14th is Bastille Day, the French National Day. It commemorates the fall of the Bastille prison to the Revolutionaries in 1789. It is a bank holiday with a military parade on the Champs-Elysées in Paris and street parties and firework displays all over France.

The national anthem, *la Marseillaise*, is a battle march composed during the French Revolution by a soldier, Rouget de Lisle, to inspire the troops. Revolutionaries from Marseille sang it on their way to Paris, giving it its name. The first lines go: *Allons enfants de la patrie, Le jour de gloire est arrivé!* Just right before a football match!

"Liberté, Egalité, Fraternité", the motto of the Revolution, represents the values the French Republic strives to maintain, more or less successfully. It features on public buildings and on coins and stamps.

1 Read the information on pages 6 and 7 and do the quiz. Explain your answers.

   a What does *RF* stand for?

   b What do the three colours of the flag symbolise?

   c Why is France's National day on July 14th?

   d Is French spoken only in France?

2 Using a dictionary, work out the meaning of the first two lines of *La Marseillaise* and translate them into English.

3 Choose a topic and write a short paragraph in English.

   a Sum up the French symbols and explain what symbolises Britain.

   b Should the French keep a war song as their national anthem? Make a case for or against.

   c Do you think it is important to keep regional languages alive as in France? Why?

Meet Lucas Martin's family! Four generations have gathered for a wedding *(un mariage)*. Last time they all met was for great-grandfather Martin's funeral *(les obsèques)*. They will soon meet up again for a christening *(un baptême)* and a first communion *(une première communion)*. Such family occasions usually involve a festive meal and catching up with distant relatives *(les parents)*. Family gatherings are popular with 90% of French people. 75% of 11-19 year-olds find their family life "pleasant and relaxed" and for 90%, their family is the most important thing in life.

Family names

The most common French surname is *Martin*

Other common French surnames are based on:

- Christian names: *Thomas*, *Richard*
- Places: *Laforêt*, *Deschamps*
- Occupations: *Meunier*, *Boulanger*, *Leclerc*, *Maréchal*, *Lévêque*
- Personal characteristics: *Lebrun*, *Lejeune*, *Petit*

Let's see how typical Lucas' family is.

Monsieur and Madame Martin have three children, Lucas, 13, his sister, Chloé, 19, and little brother Thomas, 2. This is slightly above the national average of 1.77 children! Only 8% of French families have three or more children.

They have a dog. More than half of French households keep a pet. In fact, France has the record number of pet owners in Europe. Their favourites are dogs, cats, fish, birds and rodents.

Lucas' grandparents live close by and often come round to help. Two-thirds of French grandparents live less than 20 kms away and are involved in their children's and grandchildren's lives.

A day with the Martins

7.00 am Lucas' day starts with the smell of fresh coffee. After kissing each other good morning, the family have breakfast together.

8.00 On his way to work, Monsieur Martin drives Chloé to the bus stop. Like most French students, she goes to the university nearest to her home. Young people leave home later than in the UK, (at age 25 on average), as they are either studying or unemployed before then.

8.30 Lucas rides his bike to school. Madame Martin drops the toddler at *la crèche municipale*, an income-related State nursery, on her way to the office where she works part time. More than 75% of French mums go out to work.

12.30 Except for Chloé, the Martins go home for their two-hour lunch break. It used to be quite common for school children to go home for lunch, but nowadays not many parents are home at lunchtime so a lot of pupils (60%) eat in the school canteen. The system of bringing a packed lunch does not exist in France.

16.40 Lucas gets back from school. He has a snack *(un goûter)*, does his homework and then plays on his computer or watches TV until dinnertime. In France, 2-19 year olds spend an average of 3 hours 30 a day in front of the TV.

19.00 Monsieur Martin comes home from work and cooks the dinner. This is quite unusual as French dads tend to do far less housework (1 hour 59 a day) than mums (3 hours 48)!

20.00 Monsieur Martin plays table football with Lucas. Most French parents spend about 12 hours a week playing with their children.

21.00 The family watches a film on the TV set in the sitting room.

22.30 Bedtime for Lucas who kisses everyone goodnight before going up.

Words young French people would use to describe their relationship with their parents:

- respect (42%)
- friendship (29%)
- lack of understanding (22%)
- conflict (6%)

1 Read the information on pages 8 and 9 and do the quiz. Explain your answers.

  a Do French people like family occasions?

  b Do the French tend to have large families?

  c Do French men and women share housework equally?

  d What sort of relationship do most French children have with their parents?

2 Look up in a dictionary the meaning of the French surnames mentioned. Can you find English equivalents?

3 Choose a topic and write a short paragraph in English.

  a Sum up the similarities and differences between the Martin family and yours.

  b Should young people live at home with their parents as long as possible as they do in France? Make a case for or against.

  c Do you think it is a good thing to have meals together as most French families do? Why?

The most spectacular changes in French society over the last few decades are probably those that have affected the traditional nuclear family, a trend very similar to that in Britain.

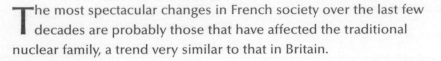

The number of married couples fell radically after the 1960s (it seems to have increased again over the last few years). The French get married much later than they used to: at the age of 28 for women and 30 for men. They have children later too. Over 90% of couples live together before marriage *(le mariage)*.

One in three or four marriages ends in divorce *(le divorce)*. In two thirds of cases, divorced couples have children and in 80% of cases the children stay with their mother. However, the number of divorces is stabilising.

In France, one in six couples live together but are not married *(vivre en cohabitation* or *en union libre)*, the second highest number in Europe after Sweden, and one in three children are now born to unmarried couples.

In 1999, after much social debate and controversy, a new contract was created in France: the PACS *(le pacte civil de solidarité)*. It gives two people, including homosexual couples, who have lived together for more than two years, the same rights and benefits as married couples. A new word was coined, *"se pacser"* (to get *"pacsed"*, i.e. to live together "officially").

The number of people staying single is increasing: over 30% of those born in the 1970s are single.

According to recent statistics, the number of weddings and divorces is stabilising

- More than 20 000 families apply to adopt a child every year. About 5 000 children are adopted (4 000 come from abroad, mainly from Vietnam).
- 63% of grandparents see their children and grandchildren at least once a week.
- 88% of young people would like to have their own family.

Le livret de famille

Whether the parents are married or unmarried, each family has a family booklet. This official family record has details of the mother and father and each child's full name, date and place of birth, as well as of death if it happens before they reach 18.

15% of young French people under 19 live with only one parent – their mother, in 80% of cases. There has been a sharp rise in the number of one-parent families *(les familles monoparentales)*, making up over 7% of households. About 45% of women in one-parent families are divorced, 20% are widows and 30% have never been married. Teenage pregnancies are increasing despite the fact that abortion was made legal in 1975 and free in 1983.

About 2% of families are made up of a couple (divorced or separated and remarried or living together) and a child or children from another marriage *(les familles recomposées)*. There are more children in these families than in traditional nuclear families, where the average number of children is two or less.

16% of French couples live separately and have a "long-distance" relationship, usually for professional reasons.

French people have been having fewer children and the population is growing older. To improve the birthrate, the State gives Family allowance *(les allocations familiales)* to any family with two or more children. Many other types of benefit are also available: "young child" allowance, "new school year" allowance, etc. and families with three or more children benefit from various discounts: public transport, cinemas, etc. Large families are even given a medal every year on Mother's Day: bronze for four or five children, silver for six or seven and gold for eight or more!

1 Read the information on pages 10 and 11 and do the quiz. Explain your answers.

   a Have French people tended to marry more or less over the last decades?

   b Is the divorce rate higher or lower than decades ago?

   c How many children have unmarried parents?

   d How many children are there in a typical French family?

2 Sketch your family tree and use a dictionary to label it in French. Try to include all the relatives you know. How far back can you go?

3 Choose a topic and write a short paragraph in English.

   a Write a description of a typical French family, based on the facts and figures given here.

   b Make a case for or against living separately because of the parents' jobs, as more than 1 in 6 of French families do.

   c Do you think the PACS is a good thing? Why?

% of people who own the following:		
	1970	**2000**
vacuum cleaner		
(Un aspirateur)	64%	97%
fridge		
(Un réfrigérateur)	80%	99%
freezer		
(Un congélateur)	6%	48%
washing machine		
(Un lave-linge)	57%	97%
tumble dryer		
(Un sèche-linge)	–	24%
dishwasher		
(Un lave-vaisselle)	3%	44%
microwave oven		
(Un four à micro-ondes)	–	63%
toaster		
(Un grille-pain)	15%	67%

French people used to spend more money on food than on their home, but during the 1990s all that changed. The average household now spends a quarter of its income on rent, heating and light and a further 6.5% on furniture, repairs and so on. People are spending more and more of their free time at home and like their home to be comfortable and well equipped.

The **kitchen** *(la cuisine)* is often the heart of a French home and new homes are designed with larger kitchens than in the past. Most kitchens are well equipped. A large number of French teenagers (80%) have their meals in the kitchen and visitors are often invited to sit round the kitchen table for a drink and a chat. A veranda *(une véranda)* or a balcony *(un balcon)* are also popular places to eat and socialise. Underneath a house there is often a **cellar** *(une cave)*, traditionally used to store wine but also a useful place to keep bikes or garden tools.

J'habite à Saint-Omer, dans le nord de la France. Chez moi, il y a une grande cuisine, un séjour, une salle de bains et trois chambres. Il y a aussi un garage et un petit jardin derrière la maison.

Claire, 14 ans

Say it with flowers

56% of French homes have a **garden** (*un jardin*).

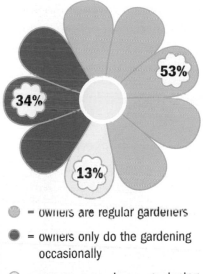

53%

34%

13%

- ⬤ = owners are regular gardeners
- ⬤ = owners only do the gardening occasionally
- ◯ = owners never do any gardening

A French **living-room** (*un salon* or *un séjour*) is typically equipped with a TV, a stereo and/or radio and a sofa and armchairs. Particularly in warmer parts of the country, there may be a rug rather than a fitted carpet.

It's becoming increasingly popular to have an **office** or **study** (*un bureau*) at home. Home computers are popular in France but not as popular as they are in Britain. One in five homes uses France-Télécom's Minitel service. With a special free Minitel terminal in their home, telephone subscribers can find out what's on at the cinema, check train or bus timetables and buy tickets.

A French **bathroom** (*la salle de bains*) may be equipped with a central mixer tap at the washbasin and a bidet, as well as a shower and/or bath. One in five French homes has more than one toilet and one in ten has more than one bathroom.

A French **garage** (*le garage*) is often part of the main house. Quite a lot of people go into their house through the garage rather than the front door. All sorts of things are stored there including food supplies (tins, jars, etc.) and, of course, the car.

1 Read the information on pages 12 and 13 and do the quiz. Explain your answers.
   a Where in the home might people sit if they wanted to eat outdoors?
   b Do you think *Minitel* might have been the reason some people do not use the Internet?
   c What is the French word for bathroom?
   d Are the French keen on gardening?
2 Using a dictionary, list in French the rooms you have in your house. Then write a list of the French names for household appliances (see page 12) in order to show how useful you think they are. Start with the most useful.
3 Choose a topic and write a short paragraph in English.
   a Make a list in English of similarities and differences between your home and a typical French home.
   b Are French homes better designed/equipped than English homes? Give reasons for your answer.
   c How do the differences between French and British homes reflect differences in French and British lifestyles?

Second homes

Some people have not just one but two homes. France is the European country with the highest proportion of second (or holiday) homes (les résidences secondaires):

- 56% are in the country (à la campagne)

- 32% are at the seaside (au bord de la mer)

- 16% are in the mountains (à la montagne).

56% of all French people live in a house (une maison individuelle) compared to 83% in Britain. That means it is quite common for a French teenager to live in a flat (un appartement). It is also more usual in France than in Britain for families to rent accommodation, although just over half of French households do own their home.

It is difficult to say what a typical French home looks like because there is so much variety. As people have always tended to use local materials to build their homes, house styles and materials vary from region to region. You may see a lot of brick houses (des maisons en briques) in the north, wooden chalet-style houses (des chalets) in the Alps or grey stone houses (des maisons en pierre grise) in Provence in the south of France, for example. The style of the roof (le toit) of a house is often typical of the region too: in Alsace, the half-timbered houses have steep roofs so the rain runs off whereas in sunnier Provence the flatter roofs are made of clay tiles, a practice probably started in Roman times. In Burgundy, pretty glazed tiles are often used to decorate the roof and in Normandy you can find picturesque houses with thatched roofs.

Homeless

There are half a million homeless *(les SDF = sans domicile fixe)* in France.

A priest called l'Abbé Pierre, with the help of a famous comedian Coluche, set up an organisation called *les restos du cœur*, literally 'restaurants with a heart'. They raise funds for soup kitchens to offer food to homeless people living on the streets. They also offer other services such as free hairdressers for the homeless and help with writing a CV.

In the centre of towns, apartment blocks *(les immeubles)* are often old, with fancy wrought iron balconies and shutters. Shutters *(les volets)* at the windows are a feature of most flats and houses in France, whether old or new. They are made from wood or metal. They keep the place cool in summer and warm in winter and are effective at keeping burglars out. Modern blocks can be found in some town centres though they are mainly situated on the outskirts of town. They usually have a security entryphone and number-coded locks *(un digicode)* on the street door.

City suburbs are growing all the time. In the 1950s and 60s, the French government built lots of low-rent public housing known as HLM *(habitations à loyer modéré)* to cope with housing shortages. The first HLM were mainly high-rise blocks built in clusters and have been described as concrete deserts because the planners did not provide enough shops, schools, play areas and other social facilities. The result was that these 'new towns' got a bad reputation and had lots of social problems. Recent HLM developments have been much more carefully designed and are attractive and pleasant places to live. Today, one in five French households live in an HLM.

---

1 Read the information on pages 14 and 15 and do the quiz. Explain your answers.

  a Would you be surprised if your French penfriend lived in a rented flat?

  b Do houses in the south of France look the same as those in the north?

  c Is it a good idea to have shutters at windows?

  d What is an HLM?

2 Use a dictionary to help you write a short paragraph explaining where you live. (see Claire's speech bubble on page 13 for help)

3 Choose a topic and write a short paragraph in English.

  a Are HLM a good idea? Explain the pros and cons.

  b Are soup kitchens enough to help the homeless? What else could be done in France and Britain?

French schoolchildren during their lunch break.

- **Compulsory school age:**
  6 to 16 (5 to 16 in the UK)

- **Average hours at school per week:**
  27 hours in primary, 30 hours in a *collège* (21 and 22 in the UK)

- **Average school holidays per year:**
  16 weeks (13 in the UK)

- **Average school days per year:**
  180 (190 in the UK)

Most French children start nursery school (*l'école maternelle*) at the age of $2\frac{1}{2}$ or 3. They normally stay at school all day and learn how to read a little and write their name. At 6, they move to primary school (*l'école primaire*), where reading, writing and arithmetic become important. They also start a foreign language, mostly English.

Between the ages of 11 and 14, pupils go to a secondary school (*le collège*). There is no assembly in a French school. Lessons start at 8 or 8.30 in the morning and finish at 4.30 or 5 in the afternoon. There is a morning break and an afternoon break of 15 minutes each. There is normally a two-hour break for lunch: some children (*les demi-pensionnaires*) eat at the canteen (*la cantine*), the others (*les externes*) go home. There are lunchtime clubs offering various activities.

Each pupil is given *un carnet de correspondance*, a notebook which is a link between the family and the school: it has the school rules, the timetable, information about dates and events and must be signed by parents on a regular basis.

> Je suis en quatrième au collège Jean-Moulin. Mes matières préférées sont le français et l'anglais. Je suis nul en maths! J'adore jouer au ping-pong. Mon collège est super.

Laurent, 12 ans

Subjects studied for 4 years in a collège:

French, Maths, History, Geography, *Sciences de la vie et de la terre* (Geology, Biology), Foreign languages (1 or 2), Physics, Chemistry, Technology, Art, Music, Latin or Greek, Physical Education, *Éducation civique* (citizenship)

80% of French pupils go to *un collège public*, a non-religious State school for pupils of all abilities. There are also private schools, mostly Catholic, funded by the State. Single sex and private schools with high fees are rare in France. In State schools, there is no religious education and no display of religious belief is allowed. However, in the *sixième* pupils study part of the Bible from a cultural point-of-view. French pupils do not wear a uniform.

In secondary school, lessons *(les cours)* normally last 55 minutes. When a teacher is away or if they have a free lesson *(une permanence)*, pupils can either go out of school or be looked after by a supervisor *(un(e) surveillant(e))* in a classroom or in the library *(le CDI, centre de documentation et d'information)*, where they can do their homework. They normally have homework *(les devoirs)* to do every evening. They note down the work to do in a *cahier de texte*.

French schoolchildren do not usually have school on Wednesday afternoons but they often have classes on Saturday mornings. Some schools operate a four-day week with all day Wednesday off. France is divided into three zones which have Spring and Autumn holidays at different times. The school year normally finishes at the end of June and starts again in early September for everyone.

1 Read the information on pages 16 and 17 and do the quiz. Explain your answers.

a Is *l'école maternelle* compulsory in France?

b How long is a day at a French secondary school?

c Do French pupils have packed lunch?

d Which days are not school days in France?

2 Use a dictionary to list in French the names of the subjects studied in secondary school in France.

How does that compare to your timetable?

3 Choose a topic and write a short paragraph in English.

a Sum up the differences and similarities between school life in France and in your country.

b Should French pupils wear school uniform? Make a case for or against.

c Do you think it is a good thing that State schools in France do not teach religious education? Why?

Le collège (ages 11-15)

la sixième: year 7

la cinquième: year 8

la quatrième: year 9

la troisième: year 10

Exam: *Le Brevet des Collèges*

Le lycée (ages 15-18)

la seconde: year 11

la première: year 12

la terminale: 6th form

Exam: *Le Baccalauréat*

The *Brevet des Collèges*

- **French (3 hours):**
  questions on a text, grammar and vocabulary exercises; dictation; essay

- **Mathematics (2 hours):**
  algebra, geometry, problem solving

- **History-Geography-Citizenship (2 hours):**
  questions on documents; short essay

In a *collège*, relationships with teachers can be quite formal. Issues such as homework, discipline and individual pupils' performance are discussed at the *Conseil de classe*, a meeting attended three times a year by the headteacher *(le proviseur)*, the teachers *(les professeurs)* and two pupils elected by their classmates to represent them *(les délégués de classe)*. Once a fortnight, pupils have a timetabled discussion *(l'heure de vie scolaire)* with the class tutor *(le professeur principal)* about school life and issues.

In the third term of *la troisième*, decisions about subject choices and careers *(l'orientation)* are made through a procedure involving pupils, parents and teachers. Pupils can move up a class, change course or, if they fail to reach the standards expected, repeat a year *(le redoublement)*. If they disagree, families can appeal against the decision. All schools have a specialist counsellor *(le conseiller d'orientation-psychologue)* to help pupils, parents and teachers.

Pupils do not sit any national exams until they reach the *troisième*, when they have an end-of-year written test, *le Brevet des Collèges*, in three main subjets: French, Maths and History/Geography. They are also assessed on their overall results throughout the previous two years in ten other subjects.

Pupils discussing their work with their class tutor

AVEC PHOSPHORE L'AVENIR VOUS APPARTIENT !

Du lycée aux études supérieures, pour franchir les étapes avec succès.

Conseils de **méthodes de travail**, fiches **métiers**, dossiers spéciaux sur **l'orientation** : *Phosphore* est une mine d'infos pour vos études et vos choix pour l'avenir

Et chaque mois, l'actualité, les loisirs et la culture sont au rendez-vous !

Ciné, musique, multimédia, etc : *Phosphore* dévoile des nouveautés et des talents. Les articles de décodage de l'actualité sont une véritable

PHOSPHORE

ANOREXIE
L'ivresse de la minceur

DOSSIER
LES GUERRES DU FUTUR

IRAK
Un inspecteur témoig

ENQUÊTE
Quel têtard êtes-vous ?

ÉTUDES SUP
DEVENEZ INGÉNIEUR
les filières les écoles

CONSO
L'univers de la glisse

MÉTIERS
RESSOURCES HUMAINES
Votre carrière les intéresse

Internet : www.phosphore.com

In France, the *collège* and the *lycée* are different schools, so going from one to the other usually involves many changes in pupils' lifestyle: *lycées* are often huge places (over 2000 students), sometimes far away from home (some students become boarders *(pensionnaires)* and go home only at weekends or during holidays), school days are longer (8 hours on average, with lessons on both Wednesday and Saturday mornings), subjects are more demanding with new, challenging areas, such as philosophy. There are many types of *Baccalauréat* exam to suit students' interests and abilities. During their first year, students must choose the options which will determine which type they will do at the end of the third year.

The general types are L *(littéraire)*, S *(scientifique)* and ES *(économique et social)*. There are also many vocational types such as SMS *(sciences médico-sociales)*, the most popular with girls, STI *(sciences et technologies industrielles)*, more popular with boys, etc. It is almost always necessary to have the *Bac* to go to university. The overall pass rate in France is around 80%. About 40% of French 19-21 year olds go on to further and higher education.

---

1 Read the information on pages 18 and 19 and do the quiz. Explain your answers.

a Do French pupils automatically go up a year every year?

b Do French students have to be boarders when they go to a *lycée*?

c When do pupils get a chance to express their views about school life?

d How does the *Brevet des Collèges* compare with the equivalent exam in your country?

2 Explain to an English friend what the magazine *Phosphore* is all about. Is there anything similar in Britain?

3 Choose a topic and write a short paragraph in English.

a Sum up the differences between *la seconde* and the equivalent year in Britain.

b Should some British pupils repeat a year like some do in France? Make a case for or against *le redoublement*.

c Do you think it is important to go through the process of electing *délégués de classe*? Why?

It's not all work and no play for French teenagers. As well as weekends and those long school holidays, most children have all or part of Wednesday off school. It used to be a day for religious studies but now it's used for sport, cinema outings or clubs such as scouts and guides. Between the ages of 11 and 14, there is a difference in what interests boys and girls. Boys prefer playing video games *(les jeux de console)* whereas girls choose reading *(la lecture)*, drawing *(le dessin)* or painting *(la peinture)*.

Favourite hobbies for 11–19 year olds

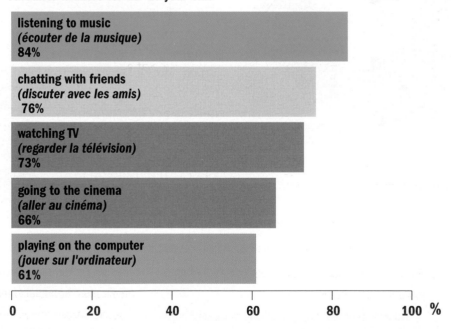

- **listening to music** *(écouter de la musique)* 84%
- **chatting with friends** *(discuter avec les amis)* 76%
- **watching TV** *(regarder la télévision)* 73%
- **going to the cinema** *(aller au cinéma)* 66%
- **playing on the computer** *(jouer sur l'ordinateur)* 61%

0   20   40   60   80   100 %

The average French teenager spends as much time watching TV as he/she does at school (about 800 hours a year). The day of the week when most TV is watched is Wednesday.

Music is the top leisure activity for French teenagers. Quite often they will listen to the same music as you. In France, British and American bands and singers are as popular as French ones. With a couple of exceptions, French pop music *(la musique pop)* has not really made it big in English-speaking countries. MC Solaar for rap *(le rap)* and Air and Daft Punk for techno *(la techno)* are probably the best known names. Good radio stations for music are NRJ, Fun Radio and Skyrock.

Where the French stay on holiday

with family or friends *(chez des parents ou des amis)*	26%
at a campsite *(au camping)*	21%
self-catering house or flat *(en location)*	16%
at a hotel *(à l'hôtel)*	5%
other *(autres)*	32%

The Paris region is the home of two great amusement parks:

Disneyland Paris at Marne-la-Vallée

Parc Astérix is based on the cartoon character.

Pendant les vacances d'été, je vais au bord de la mer, chez ma grand-mère. Je fais de la natation et je joue au volley sur la plage. En hiver, je fais du ski.

In February, schoolchildren all have two weeks' winter holiday, commonly called *vacances de ski* as many teenagers go to ski school. But July and August are the main months for time out *(le temps libre)* and holidays *(les vacances)* in France. In Paris and other large towns, a lot of small shops and restaurants close up for a whole month so that the owners can go away for a few weeks. Traffic jams can be horrendous as thousands of French holidaymakers and foreign tourists head to the coast, the most popular destination. Nine out of ten French holidaymakers *(les estivants)* prefer to stay in France rather than travel abroad in the summer. Certainly, France has something to suit everybody: seaside *(la mer)*, mountains *(la montagne)*, lakes *(les lacs)*, countryside *(la campagne)* and cities *(les cités)*.

A large number of French children – particularly between 7 and 14 – spend time at a summer camp *(une colonie de vacances)* where they are looked after by *moniteurs* who organise outings, games and activities. These camps are often subsidised by the State or the company that one or other of the parents works for. One in four teenagers stays at home during the summer holidays.

All over France, local festivals are organised during the summer months. *Le Festival InterCeltique* in Brittany attracts a quarter of a million people.

1 Read the information on pages 20 and 21 and do the quiz. Explain your answers.

a Are you surprised that Wednesday is the day most TV is watched?

b What activity is popular in February?

c Why would it be a good idea for a French family **not** to take a holiday in July or August?

d What is a *colonie de vacances*?

2 In French, list the activities mentioned on pages 20 and 21 in the order you like them and use a dictionary to add some more activities to the list.

3 Choose a topic and write a short paragraph in English.

a Do you watch more or less TV than the average French teenager? Explain the advantages and disadvantages of watching a lot of TV.

b Compare French holiday habits with those of people in your country/area.

c What are the advantages/disadvantages of *colonies de vacances*?

The French love sport *(le sport)*. Even if they don't take part themselves, they are keen spectators. France can boast a number of world-famous sporting events and the government has spent a lot of money building impressive facilities like the *Palais Omnisports de Paris-Bercy*.

Cycling *(le cyclisme)*

During the *Tour de France* cycle race, crowds line the streets as the cyclists follow a new 2500 mile route round France each summer. The finish, which is always on the Champs-Elysées in Paris around 14th July (Bastille Day), is something of a national event. The winner of the previous day's leg of the race wears a special yellow jersey *(le maillot jaune)*. Two other jerseys to spot are *le maillot vert* (a green jersey worn by the leader on points) and *le maillot à pois* (a red polka-

dot jersey worn by the 'king of the mountains' *(le meilleur grimpeur)*.

Football *(le football* or *le foot)*

Football is the most popular sport in France today. After a fabulous victory in the World Cup *(la Coupe du Monde)* in 1998, the French national team – known as *les Bleus* because of their blue jerseys – were heroes. But early defeat in the 2002 competition left their supporters disillusioned and a bit annoyed. A lot of the best French players are snapped up by foreign clubs who have more money to spend than the French clubs. *Le Championnat de France de Football* is the competition for France's 20 first-division clubs. When *Paris-Match* magazine asked the French public to vote for the greatest sportsmen/women of the last 50 years, three of the top five were footballers : Zinedine Zidane (36% of the votes), Fabien Barthez (35%) and Michel Platini (25%).

Pétanque or Boules

Although a large number of fans of this game – which is a bit like bowls – are old men in berets, it is popular with all ages. It is in fact the fourth most popular sport in France and there are local, national and international championships.

Did you know...?

- The most popular video games in France are sports based (Gran Turismo, Fifa, etc.).

- Tennis *(le tennis)* is becoming less popular but golf *(le golf)* is gaining in popularity.

- Rugby *(le rugby)* is most popular in the South-West of France. Top teams are Brive, Pau, Toulouse and Racing de Paris.

- In Brittany, with its long coastline, sailing *(la voile)* is a popular activity. The French have been successful in a lot of transatlantic yacht races.

- Surfing *(le surf)* and snowboarding *(le snowboard)* are popular sports among young people.

- Bullfights *(les corridas)* and bullraces *(les courses de taureaux)* take place in the summer months in towns in the South of France like Arles and Nîmes which have large Roman arenas.

Motor-racing *(les courses d'automobile)*

The Le Mans 24 hour car race *(les 24 heures du Mans)* takes place on a special permanent track – 16.4 km long – through the town of Le Mans in the Sarthe region of France. Each car has two or three drivers who take turns. The Monte-Carlo Rally and the Monaco Grand Prix also draw huge crowds.

Hunting and shooting *(la chasse)*

Because of its rural past and unsentimental attitude to wild animals, France has long been a hunting nation. Today there are more than 5 million hunters, more than in any other country in Europe and double the number in Britain, even though 60% of the population say they are against blood sports.

Roller-blading *(le roller)*

There are more than 4 million roller-bladers in France and the number is growing. As many as 12 000 take part in the Friday evening parades round the streets of Paris. Special parks and tracks have been built recently for the growing numbers of roller-bladers and skateboarders.

1 Read the information on pages 22 and 23 and do the quiz. Explain your answers.
   a Why do spectators look out for the colour of jersey cyclists in the Tour de France are wearing?
   b What was a high spot for French football fans?
   c Do the French approve of hunting as a sport?
   d What is the French attitude to roller-blading?

2 In French, list the sports mentioned on pages 22 and 23 in the order you like them and use a dictionary to add some more to the list.

3 Choose a topic and write a short paragraph in English.
   a Do you think blood sports such as hunting and bullfights should be allowed? Make a case for or against.
   b Should foreign clubs be allowed to buy French footballers? What are the pros and cons?

Food and drink

France is famous for its food and wines. The French are proud of their food and spend a lot of time preparing it. Eating is not just something you have to do, it is a real pleasure and a part of French culture. A lot of foreign visitors are surprised at just how long the French spend at the table, particularly for Sunday lunch or special occasion meals.

Breakfast *(le petit déjeuner)* is usually a fairly quick and simple meal: a large bowl of hot chocolate *(un chocolat chaud)*, black coffee *(un café noir)* or coffee with milk *(un café au lait)* together with a slice or two of bread and butter with jam *(des tartines)* or, at weekends, a croissant. People sometimes like to dunk their bread in their coffee. Some young people have fruit juice, cereal, yoghurt or a little sponge cake as well or instead.

Food facts

Food is still an important part of life for the French but they are spending less and less on it:

% of budget spent on food

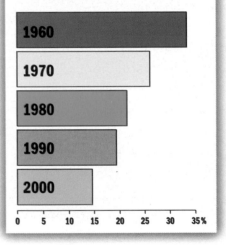

| 1960 |
| 1970 |
| 1980 |
| 1990 |
| 2000 |

0 5 10 15 20 25 30 35%

Weekday lunch *(le déjeuner)* for the French teenager is usually a meal in the school canteen *(la cantine)*; pupils don't take packed lunches. If they live near the school, some pupils will go home for lunch. The standard of school meals is generally good and there are usually three courses. When they get home at 4 or 5pm, most children have a small snack *(un goûter)* – often some bread with jam or a chocolate bar – so they won't be hungry as the evening meal is not usually until 7 or 8pm.

Dinner *(le dîner)* is usually a family meal. There might be several courses: a simple starter like grated carrots *(des carottes râpées)* or pâté, followed by a meat or fish dish with a vegetable, followed by a green salad, then cheese and fruit. There will be a jug of water and a basket of fresh bread on the table.

Average time spent eating meals per day	
breakfast	18 mins
lunch	33 mins
dinner	45 mins

> Au petit déjeuner, je mange des tartines et je bois du chocolat chaud. Le midi, je mange à la cantine du collège. J'aime le poulet et le steack-frites.

Although the French are eating less bread *(le pain)* than they did 10 years ago, it is still an important part of their diet, available at every meal. Bread is bought at the supermarket *(le supermarché)* or more commonly at the local baker's *(la boulangerie)*. There are plenty of *boulangeries* in France as people like their bread fresh and buy it every day, sometimes twice a day. There is not much brown bread. Most people buy a long French stick *(une baguette)* or an even thinner stick called *une ficelle* (literally 'string'). Bought fresh, the *baguette* smells so good most people can't resist breaking off the end to nibble on the way home. Bread is usually eaten on its own, without butter.

La France des fromages

Cheese *(le fromage)* is another staple of the French diet. It is quite common to have a cheese course before eating dessert at lunch or dinner. You won't get bored eating the same thing because there are supposed to be 362 different types of cheese produced in France, a different one for each day of the year near enough! Each region has its own special cheese. Have you tried Brie or Camembert, soft and creamy with a white crust, made from cow's milk? Roquefort is a strong flavoured cheese made from sheep's milk and there are a number of cheeses made from goat's milk. The French eat more cheese than any other nation in the world (23 kilos a person every year).

1 Read the information on pages 24 and 25 and do the quiz. Explain your answers.

a Do you think breakfast is the most important meal of the day in France?

b What is *un goûter*?

c What is different about bread in France compared to Britain?

d Is cheese more important in France or in Britain?

2 Use a dictionary to help you list in French what you eat in a typical day.

3 Choose a topic and write a short paragraph in English.

a Do you think it is a good idea to spend time preparing and eating food as the French do? What are the advantages and disadvantages?

b Should French schools allow pupils to bring a packed lunch? Give your reasons.

If you want to eat out in France, there is plenty of choice. Cafés *(les cafés)* are really for drinks, though you may be able to buy a snack *(un casse-croûte)*, such as a sandwich *(un sandwich)* or a *croque-monsieur* (toasted ham and cheese on square bread). A lot of people like to sit at a table in front of a café *(la terrasse)* and watch the world go by as they sip strong black coffee *(un express)* in tiny cups. Teenagers often meet up with friends at the café for a drink of coke or *un diabolo-menthe* (a 'mint devil' made from mixing bright green mint syrup with lemonade). Some cafés have juke boxes or table football *(le babyfoot)*. If you are in a hurry, you can stand at the counter to have a drink – it works out cheaper that way.

The standard of food is high and prices are usually reasonable in most French restaurants. Children are welcome in restaurants and a family Sunday lunch out is a common treat. There are still thousands of wonderful small family-run restaurants offering great food. The set-menu *(le menu à prix fixe)* offers the best value for money. However, as elsewhere in Europe, chain restaurants and fast-food outlets are spreading and taking away customers from the more traditional restaurants.

In the same way, supermarkets and hypermarkets have taken away customers from many of the small, specialised food shops. However, a lot of people still like to buy food, especially fruit and vegetables, at the local market *(le marché)*.

North African restaurants serving couscous (a dish of savoury semolina with meat or vegetables) and Vietnamese restaurants serving spicy dishes are the French equivalent of Indian and Chinese restaurants in Britain and are very popular.

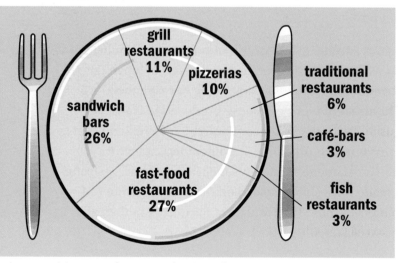

Most popular types of eating-places

Eating meat

There are not many vegetarians *(les végétariens)* in France. Uncooked meat is bought from the butcher's *(la boucherie)* and cooked meats like pâté and salami from the delicatessen *(la charcuterie)*. In many towns you can still find a rather unusual type of butcher's – *une boucherie chevaline*, which sells horse meat. You can spot it by the horse's head symbol outside.

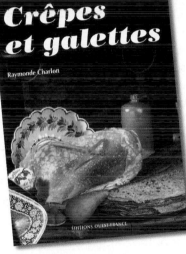

Many of the world's great wines come from France. Perhaps the most famous and one of the most expensive is champagne *(le champagne)* – the sparkling white wine for special occasions – which comes from the Champagne region of north-east France. Wine is made from grapes: green grapes make white wine *(le vin blanc)*, black grapes can make either red *(le vin rouge)* or white wine. France is lucky to have lots of wine-growing regions, like Bordeaux, Burgundy and the Loire Valley. Today, France produces and exports more wine than any other country in the world. The French drink a lot of the wine they produce themselves as well – on average, 64 litres a person every year. In Europe, only the Portugese drink more wine than the French. Twenty-five years ago, they used to drink twice as much but now quality is considered more important than quantity. Recent government campaigns have highlighted the dangers of excessive drinking (responsible for 25% of hospital admissions and 60 000 deaths a year as well as half of all road accidents).

Every region of France has its own specialities, but in a recent survey the *quiche lorraine* was voted the 'national dish'. This is a simple tart made with eggs and ham which can be eaten hot or cold. Brittany is famous for its seafood *(les fruits de mer)* and for pancakes *(les crêpes* or *les galettes)*. The *fondue savoyarde* originated in the Alps. Cheese is melted with white wine to make a gooey mixture into which you dip cubes of bread. The south of France has given us dishes like *la ratatouille* and *la salade niçoise*, and *l'andouillette* is a tripe sausage, a particular speciality of the town of Tours.

1 Read the information on pages 26 and 27 and do the quiz. Explain your answers.

a Why do French people go to cafés?

b Are traditional restaurants more popular than fast-food outlets?

c Can you get foreign food in France?

d Is wine important?

2 In French, list as many items of food and drink as you can.

See if you can come up with at least one item for each letter of the alphabet.

3 Choose a topic and write a short paragraph in English.

a Do you think we should have *boucheries chevalines* as the French do? Give your reasons.

b Explain the dangers of drinking too much wine.

c Do you think fast-food restaurants will eventually squeeze out traditional restaurants? Why?

January

1 🏳️ *Le Jour de l'An* (New Year's Day)
A festive lunch with family and friends, a visit to elderly relatives, and *des étrennes* (extra pocket money) for the children. Over the next few weeks, the French will write to send New Year greetings to people who are far away. These are often written on formal visiting cards (*des cartes de visite*).

6 ✝ *L'Epiphanie* (Twelfth Night)
Whoever finds the charm hidden in *la galette des Rois* (a flat round cake with a paper crown on it) is crowned king or queen.

February

2 ✝ *La Chandeleur* (Candlemas)
People make and toss pancakes (*les crêpes*), with a coin in their pocket for good luck!

14 *La Saint-Valentin* (Valentine's Day)
Celebrated in very much the same way as in Britain, with cards, flowers and an over-priced meal at a restaurant!

March

✝ *Mardi Gras* (Shrove Tuesday)
A time for carnivals and more pancakes, to celebrate the beginning of Lent (*le Carême*), a Christian tradition of fasting for 40 days before Easter. The *Carnaval de Nice*, with its magnificent floats, is the most famous in France and attracts thousands of visitors every year.

🏳️ = official bank holidays (*jours fériés*)

✝ = Catholic festivals

April

1 *Poisson d'Avril* (April Fool's day)
People play tricks (*des farces*) on friends and family. Children stick paper fish on people's backs and journalists invent hoaxes. Everyone says: *Poisson d'Avril!*

✝ 🏳️ *Pâques* (Easter)
On Easter Sunday, children get chocolates shaped like eggs (*les œufs de Pâques*), bells, chickens, rabbits, etc. Some families hide eggs in the garden for children to hunt. Easter Monday is a day off.

May

1 🏳️ *La Fête du Travail* (Labour Day)
A day off work. Trade Unions organise processions in towns and cities. It's also traditional for people to give a bunch of lily of the valley to family and friends for luck.

8 🏳️ *La Fête de la Victoire* (Victory in Europe Day)
To commemorate victory in World War II in 1945, there is a ceremony where officials and war veterans place flowers at the foot of the war memorial (*le Monument aux Morts*), found in most French towns.

La fête des Mères (Mother's Day)
On the last Sunday of the month, it is traditional for children to give their mum a present and for the family to go out to a restaurant. *Bonne fête, Maman!*

end May-June ✝ 🏳️ *L'Ascension*
This Catholic festival takes place 40 days after Easter. It is usually on a Thursday. Most French people tend to take the Friday off as well and have a long weekend. It is called *faire le pont* (to make a bridge).

June

mid-June *La fête des Pères* (Father's Day)
Although less celebrated than Mother's Day, it is now traditional to remember the dads by giving them a present, quite often a tie or aftershave!

✝ 🏳️ *La Pentecôte* (Whitsun)
The religious significance of this Christian festival has been forgotten, and it is seen by many as an opportunity to go away on a long weekend. It is now sadly associated with a high number of fatal road accidents, as many people are on the move.

21 *La fête de la Musique* (Music Day)
Since 1982, France has celebrated the first day of summer with street concerts and performances. This has become an extremely popular festival.

Dans ma famille, on fête Noël et le Nouvel An. En plus, on fête aussi l'Aïd: c'est une fête musulmane pour la fin du Ramadan. Nous, on aime bien faire la fête en famille!

24 *Le feu de la Saint-Jean*
(Mid-Summer's Day)
Most places in France celebrate 24th June by having a huge fire burning with food, drinks, music and sometimes fireworks.

July

Les grandes vacances (summer holidays)
School finishes at the end of June, for at least eight weeks! Lots of people set off on holiday (mainly making for the South of France).

14 🇫🇷 *La Fête Nationale* (Bastille Day)
This day commemorates the storming of the Bastille prison by French Revolutionaries in 1789. People celebrate with fireworks and street parties, on the 13th or 14th at night. The official celebration consists of a military parade on the Champs-Elysées in Paris.

August

15 † 🇫🇷 *L'Assomption* (Assumption)
Catholics honour the Virgin Mary with church services and processions in towns and villages. For most people, it has become synonymous with either a family meal or traffic jams on the way home from holiday!

September

1st week *La rentrée* (back to school)
Time for pupils to go back to school. They have bought their school equipment (pens, pencils, exercise books, etc.) and their books beforehand.

October

Festivals des Vendanges
(Grape harvest festivals)
October is the month when the grapes are picked to make wine (a backbreaking job usually done by students). Many festivals take place after the harvest in the wine growing regions.

31 *Hallowe'en*
Although an old Celtic tradition, Hallowe'en wasn't celebrated in France until recently. It is now very popular with children and has become an extremely commercialised event.

November

1 † 🇫🇷 *La Toussaint* (All Saints' Day)
Traditionally, French people visit the cemetery on this day to pay their respects and to decorate the family graves with chrysanthemums.

11 🇫🇷 *L'Armistice* (Remembrance Day)
The end of World War I is commemorated all over France. In Paris, the President of the Republic places flowers on the Tomb of the Unknown Soldier under the *Arc de Triomphe*.

December

5
In the north and the east of France, *Saint Nicolas* (Santa Claus) comes to reward good children. In other regions of France, they must wait until Christmas to get presents.

24 *Le soir de Noël* (Christmas Eve)
French people celebrate Christmas with a *réveillon* (a party with a late dinner and special food). Christians go to midnight mass.

25 † 🇫🇷 *Le jour de Noël* (Christmas day)
Children open their presents in the morning. It is usually a day for family gatherings and a traditional meal of oysters, turkey with chestnuts and a chocolate Christmas log. *Joyeux Noël!* (Merry Christmas). It is not traditional for French people to send Christmas cards. Friends, neighbours and family members don't exchange cards as they do in Britain.

31 *La Saint-Sylvestre* (New Year's Eve)
This is celebrated with another *réveillon*, often with friends or in a restaurant. At midnight, people drink a glass of champagne and wish each other *Bonne année!* (Happy New Year) under a branch of mistletoe for good luck.

Number of days off

11 days   official bank holidays (UK: 8)

104 – weekends (UK: 104)

25 paid holidays (UK: about 20 days)

140 days off work (UK: 132)

---

1 Read the information on pages 28 and 29 and do the quiz. Explain your answers.

a When can you become a king/queen in France?

b What is the 14th July?

c When do French children receive their Christmas presents?

d Are all French bank holidays religious occasions?

2 Using a dictionary, find as many French words as you can relating to Christmas in Britain (tree, presents, etc.).

3 Choose a topic and write a short paragraph in English.

a Sum up the similarities and the differences between British and French festivals.

b Should the end of WWI and WW2 still be remembered with a bank holiday in Britain as they are in France? Make a case for or against.

JUILLET			AOÛT		
Les jours diminuent de 58 mn			Les jours diminuent de 1 h 37		
1	M	Thierry	1	S	Alphonse
2	J	Martinien	2	D	Julien
3	V	Thomas	3	L	Lydie	32
4	S	Florent	4	M	J.-M. Vianney
5	D	Antoine-Marie	5	M	Abel
6	L	Marietta	28	6	J	Transfiguration
7	M	Raoul	7	V	Gaétan
8	M	Thibaut	8	S	Dominique
9	J	Amandine	9	D	Amour
10	V	Ulrich	10	L	Laurent	33
11	S	Benoît	11	M	Claire
12	D	Olivier	12	M	Clarisse
13	L	Henri/Joël	29	13	J	Hippolyte
14	M	F. NATIONALE	14	V	Evrard
15	M	Donald	15	S	ASSOMPTION
16	J	N.-D. Mt C.	16	D	Armel
17	V	Charlotte	17	L	Hyacinthe	34
18	S		18	M	Hélène

When it is your name day *(la fête)*, people wish you *"Bonne fête!"*, friends send cards and small children get a little present.

How religious are the French?

- Catholics who go to church regularly: 7%
- Catholics who go to church occasionally: 24%
- Catholics who don't go to church: 41%
- Muslims: 2%
- Jews: 1%
- Protestants: 1%
- Others: 2%
- Non-believers: 21%

What do religious festivals mean to the French?

- a chance to have a day off with family (83%)
- an opportunity to reflect on the meaning of life (48%)
- a time to go to a religious service (42%)
- a time for prayer (33%)

Catholicism has played an important role in the country's cultural heritage and traditions. There is evidence of this in everyday life, for instance in the main festivals, regional folk festivals (like the *pardons* in Brittany), the calendar, where every day is named after a saint, the architecture, the numerous places of pilgrimage (over 1500 of them, like the world-famous Lourdes), the crosses and grottos at the roadside, street names and school names, etc.

Pardons are still very popular festivals in Brittany and attract many tourists.

As religion now impacts less on lives in France, it is no longer at the heart of traditional family events: there are fewer church weddings, fewer christenings *(le baptême)* and fewer children taking their first communion *(la première communion)*.

France is Catholic by tradition. However, the population of France includes people from many religions. Islam is France's second religion with over 5 million Muslims. They have their own customs, traditions, festivals (Ramadan, Eid, etc.) and food: the North African dish, *couscous*, has become one of France's national dishes and *raï* (a mixture of old and modern North African music), one of the French young people's favourite types of music.

North African dishes such as *couscous* are very popular in France

Some French superstitions

bring good luck:

- a four leaf clover
- a ladybird landing on your finger
- breaking white glass
- seeing a spider in the evening

bring bad luck:

- walking under a ladder
- breaking a mirror
- having 13 guests at a table
- seeing a spider in the morning

France is a mixture of colourful customs and traditions which vary greatly from region to region. As in Britain, each area has its own specialities for food and meals, such as pancakes in Brittany, cheese fondue in the Alps, *cassoulet* (meat and white beans stew) in the south-west, etc.

Some regions have their own language and their own distinctive folk songs and traditional music, particularly Brittany with celtic sounds such as bagpipes, and Corsica with its polyphonic singing.

Every region of France has its traditional costumes *(les costumes traditionnels)*, now only worn during folk festivals.

A *bigouden* (south-west Brittany)

The different regions have different types of festivals and festivities.

● In Brittany, the *fest-noz* – literally "night feast", with traditional and modern celtic music, dance and food – are becoming increasingly popular.

● In the south-west of France, the *férias* (annual town festivals) are influenced by Spain, with bullfights and street races with young cows.

● In the north, near Calais, whole towns become giant fun fairs and car boot sales during *la ducasse* or *la braderie*, the most famous being the *Braderie de Lille*.

● Provence is well-known for its Christmas celebrations, spanning 40 days. There are markets *(les marchés de Noël)*, where you can find *Santons*, small figures made of clay to decorate nativity scenes, street performers, singers, travelling storytellers and plays *(pastorales)* as well as *crèches vivantes* (nativity scenes with actors) and the famous 13 desserts on Christmas Eve!

Provençal *Santons*

1 Read the information on pages 30 and 31 and do the quiz. Explain your answers.
   a Are the French generally very religious?
   b When do people wish you *"Bonne fête"* in France?
   c Where can you take part in a *fest-noz*?
   d Is it lucky or unlucky to see a spider in France?

2 Look up key words needed to describe English superstitions in French.

3 Choose a topic and write a short paragraph in English.
   a Sum up and describe what influences French customs and traditions.
   b Is it important for each region to keep its traditions? Make a case for or against.
   c Do you think it is right that in a multi-faith country like France religious festivals should be official bank holidays? Why?

Main rivers:

There are 4 different types of climate:

- = mild winters, pleasant summers, moderate rainfall throughout the year

- = cold winters, hot, stormy summers

- = cold winters with lots of snow, pleasant summers

- = mild, wet winters, hot, dry summers

High mountains, dramatic gorges, rolling hills, flat plains, forests, rivers, lakes, sandy beaches, even volcanoes ... France has got it all! France is situated at the western edge of Europe, bordered by the English Channel *(la Manche)* in the North, the Atlantic Ocean *(l'océan Atlantique)* in the West and the Mediterranean Sea *(la mer Méditerranée)* in the South.

It has a varied landscape and a moderate climate. The land is a combination of plains and mountains – low-lying in the North, West and Centre, with the mountainous regions of the Vosges in the East and the Pyrenees, the Massif Central and the Alps in the South.

Of the thousands of rivers *(les fleuves)* crisscrossing France, there are five main ones:

- the **River Seine** (776 km) is well-known as it runs through the Centre of Paris. The river is a commercial route: barges on the Seine transport oil, sand and other cargo from Paris to the coast, relieving congestion on the roads.

- the **River Loire** – France's longest river (1012 km) – runs through North-West France. During the Rennaissance, beautiful castles *(des châteaux)* were built along its banks.

- the **River Garonne** (647 km) has its source in Spain, in the Pyrenees mountains, and flows into the Atlantic at the Gironde estuary in South-West France.

- the fast-flowing **River Rhône** (812 km) has its source in a glacier in the Swiss Alps. It enters France near Geneva.

- the **River Rhine** *(le Rhin)* is 1298 km long but not all of it is in France. In eastern France it forms the border between France and Germany and continues north into Holland where it flows into the North Sea. Because it flows through industrialised areas, the river is very polluted.

> J'habite à Clermont-Ferrand, dans le Centre de la France. Dans la région, il y a d'anciens volcans comme le Puy de Dôme.

Amazing landscapes

L'Aiguille du Midi

In the Alps, near the town of Chamonix and Mont-Blanc, there are mountains that look like jagged rock needles. Technically difficult to climb, these mountains are a real challenge to climbers.

Le Pont d'Arc

In the Ardèche region, a massive natural archway, *le Pont d'Arc*, spans the River Ardèche which has carved a way for itself between the high limestone cliffs. The whole area is wild, with spectacular scenery.

La chaîne des Puys

Near the town of Clermont-Ferrand in central France is a region of extinct volcanoes. If you climb to the top of the most famous, *le Puy de Dôme*, you can look out over a whole chain of volcanoes.

Les Gorges du Verdon

Known as the 'Grand Canyon of Europe', these gorges in the south of France, are over 400 metres deep and the views are spectacular. The River Verdon has cut a series of gorges or canyons through the rock over a 21 kilometre stretch.

---

1 Read the information on pages 32 and 33 and do the quiz. Explain your answers.

   a Why is the River Seine important?

   b What do the French call the English Channel?

   c Where in France can you find extinct volcanoes?

   d What is the Ardèche region like?

2 Use a dictionary to find the French names for the geographical features mentioned in the first sentence on page 32.

3 Choose a topic and write a short paragraph in English.

   a Considering the climate in different parts of the country, explain in English where in France you would prefer to live.

   b What do you think are the advantages and disadvantages of transporting goods by river?

   c Find out more about one of the places pictured and write a short article about it in English.

Spotlight on the South of France

Every summer, more than one and a half million holidaymakers visit the Var *département* in the South of France, more than any other French *département*.

The coastal region in the South of France is known as *le Midi*. It borders on the Mediterranean Sea *(la mer Méditerranée)*. To the east is the popular tourist area of the French Riviera or *la Côte d'Azur*, with attractive landscape, sandy beaches and hot, dry summer weather. The towns of Nice, Cannes and Monte Carlo appeal to the rich and famous who settle or holiday here. Marseille, on the South coast, is the largest port in France. To the west is the Languedoc region which was developed later than the Riviera. It was originally unpopular because the land was marshy and mosquitoes bred in the pools. The beaches were difficult to get to and facilities generally were poor. In the 1970s the French government made many improvements to the Languedoc region, improving access and facilities and using insecticides to clear away the mosquitoes.

The large number of tourists that visit the South of France is great for the economy but brings with it problems of pollution and litter. The large areas of forest are vulnerable to forest fires and because so many people want to visit or live in the area there is also the problem of urbanisation – if all the land is built on, the area will no longer be as attractive to visitors.

Apart from tourism, the local economy is based on shipbuilding, oil refining and manufacturing computer equipment. Large quantities of wine, vegetables and oranges and lemons and olives are also produced in the South of France.

Guadeloupe is officially part of France

France overseas

When we think of France, we think of the *'hexagone'* that is mainland France. However, France is actually divided into 100 administrative units called *départements* and five of these are nowhere near mainland France, but they are all officially a part of France. They are overseas *départements (départements d'outre-mer, or DOM,* for short):

● **Guyana** in South America, home of the Ariane rocket base. The country is mainly covered in dense, humid equatorial forest.

● **Guadeloupe** and **Martinique** in the Caribbean. These two small tropical volcanic islands grow sugar cane and fruit and attract large numbers of tourists.

● **Réunion** island in the Indian Ocean, not far from Madagascar. *Piton de la Fournaise* is a large, live volcano on the island that erupts regularly.

In addition there are territories linked to France *(les territoires d'outre-mer, or TOM).* One of the largest areas is at the South Pole. The area is uninhabited apart from a few scientists on expeditions. Other areas are lively communities, like New Caledonia or Tahiti in French Polynesia – both nearer to Australia than they are to Europe.

---

1 Read the information on pages 34 and 35 and do the quiz. Explain your answers.

a Where is *le Midi*?

b Does the economy of the south of France rely only on tourism?

c In what way would it be true to say that there are bits of France all over the world?

d Would Martinique be more popular with holidaymakers than Guyana?

2 Use a dictionary to find the French names for as many countries as you can.

3 Choose a topic and write a short paragraph in English.

a What are the advantages and disadvantages of encouraging more tourists to areas like the South of France?

b Is France your ideal holiday destination? Give reasons why.

c Use the Internet to find out more about a French-speaking area and summarise the information.

In certain areas of France, people have a strong regional identity. They have kept alive local customs and traditions: costume *(le costume)*, festivals *(les festivals)*, dance and music *(la danse et la musique)* and sport *(les sports)*. Some even have their own language *(une langue)*, which they speak in addition to French. (More about regional languages in Chapter 1.)

The Invaders

The country we call *France* used to be known as *la Gaule* (the name was taken from a Celtic tribe who settled there – the Gauls). In the year 50 BC, Julius Caesar and the Roman army defeated the Gauls and took over the country. 500 years later, a tribe from the East, the Franks, moved in and chased out the Romans. They renamed the country with their own name, *France*. Later, the land was also invaded by the Norsemen (Vikings), who became known as the Normans.

Regional cultures

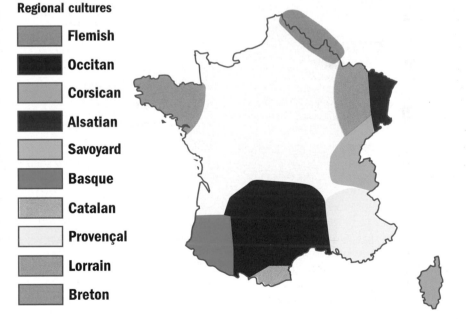

- Flemish
- Occitan
- Corsican
- Alsatian
- Savoyard
- Basque
- Catalan
- Provençal
- Lorrain
- Breton

The Breton language *(le Breton)*, for example, which is spoken in parts of Brittany, is a bit like Welsh. There are more than half a million Breton speakers and there are some Breton-speaking schools, financed by parents as they are not part of the State system, and a Breton TV channel.

People in some of these regions, like those on the island of Corsica *(les Corses)* and the Basques *(les Basques)*, would like their region to become independent of France. These independence or autonomy movements often use acts of violence to try to force the government's hand, but so far without success.

Kaixo!* J'habite à Bayonne, dans le pays basque. Je suis <u>pour</u> les traditions basques et l'autonomie mais je suis <u>contre</u> la violence.

*kaixo is the Basque word for *bonjour*

The Basque people live in the Pyrenees region. It is a mountainous area that is partly in France and partly in Spain, covering about 800 square miles. They have their own language and traditions, and they even have their own flag. The Basque name for the Basque 'nation' is *Euzkadi*.

The town of Bayonne is at the heart of the Basque country *(le pays basque)*. Every year there is a carnival *(la feria)* there in July with bullfights – reflecting the Spanish influence – and folk dancing. Special swordsticks are used in a number of Basque dances. The dances can be quite spectacular, with the dancers – mainly men wearing local costume and red berets – doing high leaps in the air.

The village of Sare has the Basque nickname *Gauazko-Lan*, which translates as *travail de nuit*, night-work. This is because it is on the French-Spanish border and in times gone by night-time smuggling was a sport, a tradition and an economic necessity.

The most popular Basque sport is the game of *pelota (la pelote basque)*. There are different versions of this centuries old game: it can be played with bare hands, with a large, curved wicker glove or with a wooden racquet. The aim is to hit a ball against a wall in order to win points. It is a fast and furious game where the ball can reach speeds of more than 100 miles an hour.

1 Read the information on pages 36 and 37 and do the quiz. Explain your answers.

  a What regional languages might you hear in France?

  b How do people in Brittany keep their local language and culture alive?

  c Where is the Basque country?

  d What is *pelota*?

2 Use a dictionary to help you make a list in French of languages spoken in France and the countries that border it.

3 Choose a topic and write a short paragraph in English.

  a Explain why the Basque country would be an interesting place to spend a holiday. If possible, use the Internet to find out more about it.

  b What do you think would be the advantages and disadvantages of regions like Corsica and the Basque country being independent from France?

Look through a French telephone directory and you will find not only traditional French surnames but also names from a wide range of origins: Italian *(italien)*, Polish *(polonais)*, Portuguese *(portugais)*, North African *(maghrébin)* and many more. Because of its history as a colonial power, its position at the heart of Europe and its wealth as a world power, France today is a multi-racial country.

Many different ethnic groups have moved to France and made it their home. France has more than 4 million immigrants *(les immigrés)*: of these, 1.3 million have taken on French nationality. It is estimated that one in four French youngsters has a parent or grandparent who was not born in France.

Before 1974, foreigners *(les étrangers)* who could find work in France were allowed to stay. In the '50s and '60s, the French encouraged them to come and work because they were glad of the cheap labour to help them industrialise the country. Immigrants often took on the poorly paid, unskilled jobs that the French did not want to do. Since then, special laws have restricted immigration rights although there are an estimated one million illegal immigrants *(les immigrés clandestins* or *les sans-papiers)*.

The French abroad

1.7 million French people live outside France:

52% in Europe

25.2% in North America

10.8% in Africa

5% in the Middle East

4.5% in Oceania

2.5% in Asia

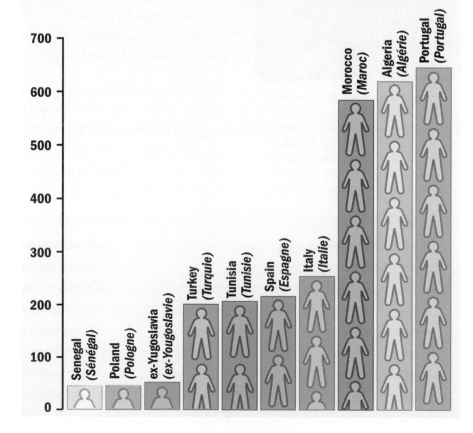

Population in thousands at the end of the 20th century originating from

North Africans from Algeria, Morocco and Tunisia, known as *les Maghrébins*, are the largest immigrant group. The French have embraced their food and their music, and young people have been influenced by their approach to fashion (baggy trousers and back-to-front baseball caps). But whereas many people of different ethnic origins live happily alongside each other in France, there is racial tension and these Arabs in particular are often the victims of racist behaviour. A young Arab is much more likely than a white youth to be stopped by the police in the street to have his or her papers checked.

In recent years, extreme right-wing political parties with racist and anti-semitic attitudes have seen an enormous rise in popularity. Some French voters still believe that immigrants are the cause of crime and high unemployment and that ethnic minority cultures are a threat to the French identity and way of life. Fortunately many young people are more tolerant and fight racism with demonstrations and slogans such as *Non au racisme!*

Résultats d'un sondage réalisé en mars 2000

● 61% des Français estiment qu'il y a trop de personnes d'origine étrangère en France.

● 52% considèrent que l'immigration est la principale cause de l'insécurité.

● 32% veulent que la France n'accueille plus d'étrangers.

France's football team is made up of players whose families originated in countries in North Africa, Central and West Africa and the Caribbean as well as mainland France. But, as in other countries, racist incidents among football supporters are common and some clubs have felt the need to start their own anti-racist campaigns.

1 Read the information on pages 38 and 39 and do the quiz. Explain your answers.

  a Why is France a multi-racial country?

  b Who are *les sans-papiers* and why do you think they are called that?

  c What is the French attitude to foreigners living in their country?

  d Which three North African countries are known jointly as *le Maghreb*?

2 Use a dictionary to help you work out the meaning of the *Résultats du sondage* (above left) and summarise the points in English.

3 Choose a topic and write a short paragraph in English.

  a Why do you think extreme right-wing parties are successful in France?

  b Compare the racist attitudes of French football supporters with those in your country. What could be done to prevent racism of this kind?

What is it about French countryside that attracts millions of visitors every year? First perhaps a feeling of space. The density of population is one of the lowest in Europe: 107 inhabitants per square kilometre, (Netherlands: 421, Belgium: 333, UK: 241, Germany: 229, Italy: 188). There are some striking differences between areas but on average, 40 % of the land has a population density of below 20 people per square kilometre.

France is not only spacious, but it also offers a great variety of landscapes: sea, mountains, forests and different types countryside. For instance, in Northern and North-Eastern France, the farmland is very flat and divided into huge regular square or rectangular fields, called *l'openfield*, mostly for growing wheat, and with very few trees.

In Central and Western France, small irregular fields are separated by hedges and trees. This type of farmland is very green and lush. It is called *le bocage*. Potatoes and all sorts of fruits and vegetables are grown here.

France Miniature
In this park, situated less than an hour south west of Paris, you can tour a miniature version of France and discover the variety of its landscapes in one day! There are 150 French landscapes to admire and over 140 mini versions of famous monuments.

Inland, Southern France is hilly, rocky, dry and bare with a special kind of vegetation (few trees and bushes) called *la garrigue*. There are few cultivated areas, mostly olive groves or vineyards and lavender or sunflowers on terraces and in valleys.

What is in a typical French village?

100 inhabitants (*un hameau*)
no services are available

100–500 inhabitants (*un village*)
a café, a school, a chapel

500–1000 inhabitants
the above + a post office, a baker, a grocer, a butcher, a church

1000–2000 (*un bourg*)
the above + a doctor, a chemist, a solicitor, a secondary school, a library, a *gendarmerie* (police), a selection of shops, weekly market

J'habite dans un village près de Toulouse. Il y a 975 habitants. C'est joli, l'air est pur mais c'est trop calme! Moi, je préfère la ville. C'est plus intéressant.

Rural France is emptying: the majority of French people prefer living in towns (there are 34 towns of 100 000+ inhabitants – see Chapter 11). However many of those who have left their village for the town do like going back to their village for holidays. There are over 31 500 villages with fewer than 2 000 inhabitants in the whole of France.

In Northern and North-Eastern France, villages often consist of a long string of houses along the main road.

In the Centre and in the West, villages are built around a chapel or a church. They tend to be quite small, with isolated houses and farms often scattered around in the nearby countryside.

A typical village in Southern and South-Eastern France is a fortified village, perched on a hilltop, with narrow streets to give protection against the sun. Another typical Southern village is a *bastide*, a medieval village designed geometrically around a central square.

Village fleuri

Created in 1959, the label Village Fleuri was originally given to villages that were decorated with flowers. It is now seen as a guarantee that the villages maintain and promote a clean and pleasant living environment.

1 Read the information on pages 40 and 41 and do the quiz. Explain your answers.

   a Are there more or less people per square kilometre in France than in Britain?

   b What sort of scenery is there in the North of France?

   c What is grown mostly in Southern France?

   d Where will you find a *bastide*? What is it?

2 Using a dictionary, list the names in French of the different services in a village in the order of importance to you.

3 Choose a topic and write a short paragraph.

   a What makes France an attractive country to visit?

   b Read Lucas' bubble. Make a case for and against living in a village.

   c Do you think it is good that the French government gives out the *Village Fleuri* label? Why?

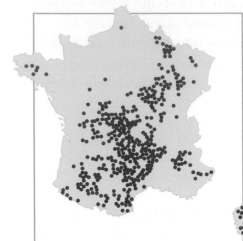

The French desert

The map shows the most empty regions in France: they follow a diagonal line *(la diagonale du vide)*, going from the North East to the South West (mostly inland and mountain areas).

French farming: facts and figures

- 80% of France is rural, 55% is farmland currently in use, 6% farmland not in use and 28% forests.

- France produces a great variety of products thanks to the diversity of soils and climates.

- French farmers are more productive than anywhere else in Europe (27% of European production).

- France is the second-largest exporter of agricultural foodstuffs in the world after the US.

Just 60 years ago, 75% of the population lived in the countryside. Most of them were farmers. Now, less than 20% of French people live in rural areas. People left villages in search of work. Many services were no longer needed and closed down. The few remaining inhabitants moved away, leaving some areas deserted (see map). However, this movement *(l'exode rural)* didn't affect all villages. Some, nearer the towns, have seen their population increase since the 1980s. About 2.5 million people, now called the *"rurbains"*, a combination of *ruraux* (rural) and *urbains* (urban), have settled in villages and commute to town for work. As new technology allows people to work from home *(le télétravail)*, the differences in lifestyles between town and country dwellers are getting blurred.

A new "rurban" estate

Only one in four people living in the countryside works the land (about 4% of the total working population). The number of farms decreases by 3-5% every year: there are 680 000 now (424 000 full time) compared with 1.6 million in 1970. In difficult times, French farmers feel undervalued and demonstrate their discontent by dumping products on the road or in front of official buildings. They receive subsidies from the European Union, sometimes making up 30%-80% of their income. Many farmers have diversified their activities by turning to tourism and inviting visitors to experience rural life (B&B, *gîtes*, camping on the farm, sale of farm products, etc.).

The French see the countryside as one of their country's great assets. In less than 15 years, 40 000 private associations for the protection of nature were created. Although half the population say they feel strongly about this issue, less than 3% actually joined. The Green Party, *les Verts* or *Écologistes*, is popular locally but only gets 5-8% of votes in general elections.

France's main protected species

- wolves (Alps)
- bears (Pyrenees)
- horses and flamingoes (Camargue)
- stags (Corsica)

To conserve France's natural heritage, 7 national parks, 29 regional parks and 128 nature reserves were created, covering nearly 10% of the land. France has the most diverse flora and fauna in Europe which need protecting from environmental dangers, such as repeated oil slicks along the Atlantic coasts, nitrates in rivers, frequent forest fires in Provence, toxic waste in industrial areas, etc. Most of the 22 billion euros the State spends on the protection of the environment goes on waste disposal.

The French government is committed to preventing mass tourism from endangering the environment and to respecting nature, local people and local economy and traditions.

◄ Since 1970, operation *"Vacances Propres"* has helped keep France clean throughout the summer months by providing over 60 000 bins in more than 1 250 tourist sites.

► Tourism: a blessing for the economy, or a curse for the environment?

1 Read the information on pages 42 and 43 and do the quiz. Explain your answers.

  a Do more French people live in towns or in the country?

  b Is the number of French farmers increasing or decreasing?

  c What does France export the most of after the US?

  d Where can you find bears in France?

2 Use a dictionary to translate into French the names of endangered animals, those in the text and others that you know of.

3 Choose a topic and write a short paragraph in English.

  a Sum up the measures taken by the French government to protect the environment.

  b As tourism puts certain areas at risk, are operations such as *"Vacances propres"* enough or should some sites be closed to visitors? Make a case for or against.

  c Would you be more prepared than the majority of French people to join an environmental group? Why?

As you enter a French town, you will see the name on a sign at the side of the road.

When you leave the town, you will see a similar sign with a diagonal line crossing out the name.

Names of streets in town are usually on blue metal plaques like this:

There are about 50 large towns in France (with 100 000 or more people living there). Of these, Paris is by far the largest (more than 10 million people live in the Paris region). After Paris come Lyon, Marseille and Lille-Roubaix-Tourcoing, each with a population of just over 1 million.

The heart of a French town may be the 'old town' (*la vieille ville* or *les vieux quartiers*), an area of narrow winding streets, sometimes dating back to the Middle Ages. In some towns it is the main square (*la grande place*), often with a cathedral (*une cathédrale*), a large church (*une église*) or a monument (*un monument historique*). In others, as in most towns in Britain, the high street (*la grande rue* or *la rue principale*) is at the heart of the town centre (*le centre ville*).

Most French towns have a market (*un marché*) once or twice a week. Sometimes part or all of the market may be in a covered hall, but French markets are mostly open-air, with stalls set up in a square or in streets throughout the town. There is always an interesting range of food stalls. Lots of French people go to market for fresh fruit and vegetables, but you can also find stalls devoted to nothing but cheese, for example, or live animals like rabbits or chickens, as well as clothes, kitchen gadgets and the like.

> Je viens en ville le samedi. Au centre ville, il y a des cafés et des restaurants, deux cinémas, une salle de concert, une piscine, et toutes sortes de magasins. Je préfère les grands magasins.

The red 'cigar' sign helps you spot the tobacconist's *(le tabac)* The sign is called *une carotte*, and dates from the days when people used to roll their tobacco into a carrot shape. If you can't find a post-office, you can buy stamps here.

The green cross is found outside the chemist's *(la pharmacie)*.

The feather sign is for the newsagent's or stationery shop *(la maison de la presse or la papeterie)*.

Shops in France often line a long, wide street known as *un boulevard*. Nowadays, though, it is quite common for shopping areas in French towns to be for pedestrians only *(des rues piétonnes)*. You can sit at a table on the terrace *(la terrasse)* in front of a café or bar and watch the world go by. The café is a French institution with young and old alike and in a French town you will never be far away from one.

Although you will find supermarkets *(les supermarchés)* and department stores *(les grands magasins)* in all French towns, and enormous hypermarkets *(les hypermarchés)* in retail parks on the outskirts of towns, France has an impressive range of small, independent shops. Many specialist shops reflect typical French preoccupations: delicious cake shops *(les pâtisseries)*, chocolate shops *(les chocolatiers)*, cheese shops *(les fromageries)*, delicatessens *(les charcuteries)* and perfume shops *(les parfumeries)*.

As well as banks, post offices, stations and bus stations, most medium to large French towns have a range of entertainment facilities: cinema, theatre, swimming pool, library, museum and so on. Some may also have a bowling alley, a skating rink or skateboard park.

If you visit France, you can get information about the town you are in from the tourist office *(l'Office de tourisme or le Syndicat d'Initiative)*. And if you are sending postcards home, remember that postboxes *(les boîtes aux lettres)* are yellow and a rectangular shape.

1 Read the information on pages 44 and 45 and do the quiz. Explain your answers.

   a Which is the largest town in France?

   b What is *un marché*?

   c Name two places you could buy stamps in France.

   d How would you recognise a chemist's shop?

2 In the paragraph above starting "As well as banks...", there are the names of various places in a French town. List the French equivalents, using a dictionary to help you.

3 Choose a topic and write a short paragraph in English.

   a In what ways is a typical French market the same as/different from markets in your country?

   b How do pedestrian shopping areas benefit French town centres?

   c What are the advantages of small, specialist shops like those in France over large stores?

French cities such as Nantes are developing fast

75% of French people live in towns, and yet towns cover only 30% of the surface area of the country. The *Ile-de-France* region, around Paris, has always been the most densely populated, despite the government's efforts in the past to attract people to live in other areas to balance things out *(les métropoles d'équilibre)*. Today more than 10 million people live in Greater Paris (compared to 7.5 million in Greater London), making it the largest city in Europe.

French people have always been attracted to Paris, but other cities – Nantes, Toulouse, Montpellier, Aix-en-Provence, for example – are also growing. Rising property prices in city centres have forced many people to move out to the suburbs *(la banlieue)*. The suburbs grew up between the two World Wars of the last century when town planners had to find ways of extending living accommodation in the towns. Architects like Le Corbusier thought that building upwards *(la construction en hauteur)* would allow green spaces *(les espaces verts)* to be protected. Large concrete cities of tower blocks *(les grands ensembles)* were built on the outskirts of many towns. From the start, there were social problems in these 'new towns' and today crime rates in many of these suburban areas are alarmingly high.

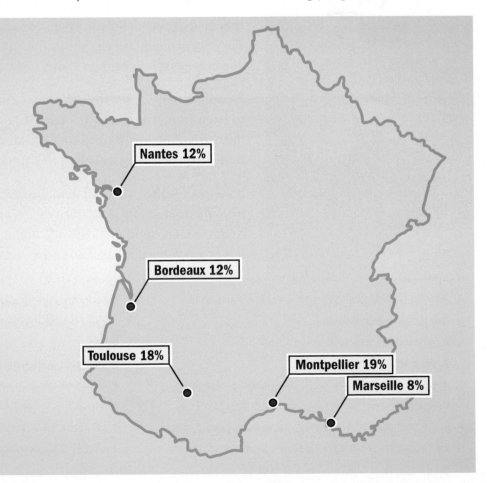

Ideal towns

In a survey in 2000, French people were asked to name the town they would most like to live in.

Here are the top 5:

Montpellier	19%
Toulouse	18%
Bordeaux	12%
Nantes	12%
Marseille	8%

Nantes 12%

Bordeaux 12%

Toulouse 18%

Montpellier 19%

Marseille 8%

Famous French towns

Strasbourg

Strasbourg, in the east of France, near the German border, is the capital of the Alsace region. It is an important river port on the Rhine and home of the Council of Europe (*le Conseil de l'Europe*) and of the European Parliament (*le Parlement Européen*). Traditionally a city of art and learning, more recently the city has made a name in the field of genetic engineering (*le génie génétique*).

Avignon

Avignon is famous for its bridge – immortalised in the song *Sur le Pont d'Avignon* – and for papal history (between 1309 and 1403 the Popes lived here). But today when French people think of Avignon it is as the setting for an international festival, an important annual event in European theatre. The old courtyards and buildings are used as stages for the performances.

Mont-Saint-Michel

Today it's a tourist trap, with souvenir-sellers lining the little streets that climb up to the Abbey, but a thousand years ago it was a place of pilgrimage. The little town grew up around the fortified Abbey (*l'Abbaye*). The mount is actually a small island which you reach by a raised road.

Cannes

Cannes is in the South of France, on the French Riviera. It is a sophisticated town in a scenic location, the setting for the glamourous Cannes Film Festival. The *Croisette* is the fashionable boulevard which divides the beach from the luxury hotels, exclusive shops and art galleries. In the old port (*le Vieux Port*), luxury yachts and fishing boats are moored side by side.

1 Read the information on pages 46 and 47 and do the quiz. Explain your answers.
 a Do French people prefer to live in towns or in the country?
 b What is *la banlieue*?
 c Why did Le Corbusier favour *la construction en hauteur*?
 d Name 3 things for which the town of Avignon is famous.
2 Write 10 key words in French for the town where you live, using a dictionary if necessary.

Example: *touristique, bruyant, musée d'art moderne...*

3 Choose a topic and write a short paragraph in English.
 a Strasbourg or Avignon – where would you prefer to live? Why?
 b Use the Internet/the library to find out more about Le Corbusier and his work.
 c Why do you think those living on estates of suburban tower blocks the French sometimes refer to as *les "quartiers"* have so many social problems?

Paris: facts and figures

Population of central Paris:
just over 2 million

Population of the Paris region:
just over 10 million (= approx 18% of the French population)

Number of visitors:
20 million+ every year

Area of central Paris:
105 square km

Area of Paris region:
just over 12 000 square km

Highest point:
Montmartre (130 metres)

Number of people who use the underground (*le métro*):
approx 5 million every day

Paris is the capital of France, by far its largest and most important city. Some people consider it to be the most beautiful city in the world. Tourists flock to Paris to see monuments like the Eiffel Tower *(la Tour Eiffel)*, which has become a symbol of the city (and of France!). Strange to think that when it was built in 1889, many Parisians *(les Parisiens)* thought the 320 metre-high tower – at that time the tallest building in the world – an ugly monstrosity! Today you can climb up the steps of the Eiffel Tower or ride up to the top in a lift to get a great view of the city.

The *Champs-Elysées* is the name of perhaps the most famous street in Paris. It is a long, wide boulevard lined with shops, cinemas, cafés and restaurants. At one end, the centrepoint of a 'star' of twelve roads, is the large arch known as the *Arc de Triomphe*, built to commemorate Napoleon's victories in battle. Further down is the Elysées Palace *(le Palais de l'Elysée)*, the impressive home of the French President.

The longest street in Paris is the *rue de Vaugirard*: 4360 metres long.

There are reminders of Napoleon all over Paris. The giant stone pillar or obelisk *(l'obélisque)* that stands in the centre of the *Place de la Concorde* (a large square at the far end of the *Champs-Elysées)* was brought from Egypt by Napoleon. Napoleon's body is in the *Hôtel des Invalides* (an old military hospital and museum) in Paris. You can visit it but don't expect to see the body as it is placed inside a series of sturdy coffins.

A Paris, j'ai vu la Tour Eiffel, j'ai visité le tombeau de Napoléon aux Invalides et j'ai passé un après-midi à la Cité des Sciences à La Villette. Aujourd'hui, je fais les magasins. C'est super !

You can get a feel of old Paris if you climb the steps up to the Sacré-Cœur church (*la Basilique du Sacré-Cœur*) and walk through the little cobbled streets around the *Place du Tertre* in Montmartre. In the past, artists like Toulouse-Lautrec and Picasso came here to paint. Nowadays, artists still come to the pretty square to sell their paintings and draw portraits of tourists.

One of the best collections of art in the world is in the Louvre Art Gallery in Paris. This is where you can see the Mona Lisa (called *La Joconde* in French). The main building was a royal palace before it became a museum after the French Revolution. The Louvre combines new architecture with old: when an extension was needed a huge, ultra-modern, glass pyramid was constructed adjoining the old palace covering a new underground entrance.

The River Seine

The Seine flows through the centre of Paris. A boat trip is a good way to see the sights without getting tired feet. There are two islands in the river: the *Ile-Saint-Louis* and the *Ile de la Cité* home of the famous Notre-Dame Cathedral which took over 80 years to build.

There are plenty of other modern sights to see in Paris, for instance:

● the Georges-Pompidou Centre (1977) – also known as *Beaubourg* – is a centre for contemporary art and culture, unusual because all the pipes and escalators are on the outside of the building

● the *Géode* is a giant sphere housing a cinema which is part of the *Cité des Sciences et de l'Industrie* at *La Villette*

● *La Grande Arche*, a giant arch, which is part of the sky-scraper district of *La Défense* in the West of Paris (a large modern development of offices and shops).

1 Read the information on pages 48 and 49 and do the quiz. Explain your answers.

   a Where does the French President live?

   b Name 3 places in Paris connected with Napoleon.

   c What is there in Paris for art-lovers?

   d How is the Pompidou Centre different from other buildings?

2 Translate into English the speech bubble at the top of the page. Use a dictionary to help you.

3 Choose a topic and write a short paragraph in English.

   a Would you rather visit the Eiffel Tower or the Louvre? Why?

   b Does Paris deserve to attract so many tourists?

   c Use the Internet/the library to find out more about one of the places mentioned and summarise what you learn.

As well as being a tourist destination, Paris is also a cosmopolitan city where people live and work. It is the seat of government and a centre for commerce and industry. 65% of France's banks and corporate headquarters are in Paris. The fact that everything centres on Paris has proved a problem for the rest of the country which has often missed out politically, commercially and culturally.

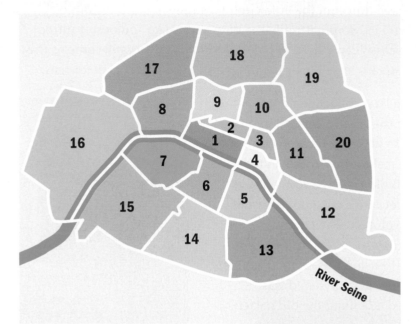

Paris is divided into 20 administrative districts of equal size (called *arrondissements*). These are numbered: 1er, 2e, 3e, etc. Street signs in Paris show which *arrondissement* you are in. As in most large cities, there are social contrasts. Traditionally, districts in the West, with wide avenues and open spaces, attract the well-off middle-classes. The Eastern *arrondissements* are more likely to be the home of the working-class or immigrants. These areas are known as *les quartiers populaires* and homes there are more modest. Eastern districts are also home to wholesale trade businesses and light industry.

Paris parks

In the city centre, parks, such as the *Tuileries* and the *Jardin de Luxembourg*, are quite small and rather formal (you are not allowed to sit on the grass!). The *Bois de Boulogne* and the *Bois de Vincennes* are large parks on the edge of the city.

Places North of the River Seine are often said to be on the *rive droite* (Right Bank) and those South of the river on the *rive gauche* (Left Bank). The Latin Quarter *(le Quartier Latin)* on the Left Bank is the student quarter. A third of France's university students study at the world-famous Sorbonne, France's oldest university. The Latin Quarter is a lively, colourful part of town, full of North African, Vietnamese and Greek restaurants, bars, cafes, bookshops and markets.

Art and the metro

- The stations of *Abbesses* and *Porte Dauphine* have Art-Nouveau entrances made from swirls of green metalwork:

- *Bastille* station has a ceramic fresco with scenes copied from newspaper engravings published during the French Revolution.

- At *Louvre-Rivoli* station, there are statues, photos and bas-reliefs to remind travellers of the works of art in the Louvre museum outside.

Paris has a quick, efficient and inexpensive public transport system *(les transports en commun)*. The underground *(le métro)* – see also page 55 – is the most popular form of transport. With more than 300 *métro* stations across the city, there is usually one nearby. A flat-price ticket is valid for any length of journey and can also be used on buses. In addition to the *métro*, there are 56 bus routes in the capital.

For slightly longer journeys, there is the RER *(Réseau Express Régional)*. This express underground service has trains to and from the suburbs. It cuts across the city centre and is faster than the regular *métro* and the stops are further apart. The RER was created jointly by the RATP *(Régie Autonome des Transports Parisiens)* which runs the *métro* and the buses and the SNCF *(Société Nationale des Chemins de fer Français)*, the national organisation that runs the railways.

However, despite the excellent public transport provision, roads in Paris are usually congested and air pollution from traffic is a major environmental hazard. The government has taken steps to encourage Parisian motorists to leave their cars at home on specially designated days, although these have met with limited success. There is also a ring road *(le périphérique)* which runs round the edge of the central area of the city.

1 Read the information on pages 50 and 51 and do the quiz. Explain your answers.
   a What is an *arrondissement*?
   b Where in Paris are there a large number of students?
   c Why is the *métro* a popular form of transport?
   d Is it a good idea to travel by car in Paris?
2 Make a list in French of vehicles/forms of transport you might find in Paris (include those mentioned above and others: e.g. *les vélos*, etc.). Use a dictionary to find any words you do not know.
3 Choose a topic and write a short paragraph in English.
   a Compare public transport in Paris with the services in your town.
   b In what way do you think other parts of France suffer if all resources are centred on Paris?
   c Is it a good idea to have special days where drivers have to leave their cars at home as they do in Paris?

French firts

French firsts

The Montgolfier brothers invented the hot-air balloon in 1783.

In 1909, French aviator Louis Blériot was the first person to fly across the Channel.

In France, there are...

- Roads (*les routes*): 1 500 000 km
- Railways (*les chemins de fer*): 34 600 km
- Rivers (*les rivières et les fleuves*), and canals (*les canaux*): 8 600 km

Concorde, the fastest passenger plane in the world

Travelling around France is easy as it has the longest road, rail and canal network in Europe.

The national airline, *Air France*, transports 14 million passengers a year. Most people arrive at one of the main Paris airports – *Roissy-Charles-de-Gaulle* or *Orly*. The supersonic jet, *Concorde*, was built jointly by French and British companies. With a journey time of less than 4 hours between Paris and New York, it is the fastest passenger plane in the world.

Ferries (*les ferries*) and hovercraft (*les aéroglisseurs*) from French ports like Calais, Boulogne and Le Havre cross the Channel (*la Manche*) linking France with Britain, although many people prefer to travel under the Channel. Opened in 1994, the Eurotunnel joining the two countries is the longest rail tunnel in the world.

> Je vais au collège à vélo ou en voiture. Le samedi, je vais chez ma copine à pied ou je vais en ville en bus.

Delphine, 13 ans

People drive on the right-hand side of the road in France. The French tend to drive French-produced cars *(les voitures)*. Renault, Peugeot and Citroën are all very popular. The last two numbers on a car's number-plate tells you the *département* the driver comes from (75 = central Paris, for example).

You have to pay to use most motorways *(les autoroutes)*. The sign *Péage* indicates there is a toll. Anyone over 14 can ride a moped *(une mobylette)* and teenagers often use them to get to school.

If you drive in France, you need to know that you must give way to traffic coming from the right at junctions *(la priorité à droite)*. Don't miss traffic lights *(les feux rouges)* which are often high above the middle of the road. Lights go straight from red to green. Amber only shows <u>before</u> the lights go red. Pedestrians *(les piétons)* should remember that it is not obligatory for cars to stop at pedestrian crossings. Every day, 22 people are killed on French roads. A third of these fatal accidents involve a driver over the alcohol limit and in half the cases the driver was speeding.

You can travel by bus *(le bus* or *l'autobus)* in towns. You punch your ticket *(un billet* or *un ticket)* in a machine on the bus as you get on. In country areas, the bus is usually a coach *(un car)*.

Types of road

Motorways *(les autoroutes)*:
A1, A2 etc

A roads *(les routes nationales)*:
N34, N35 etc

Secondary roads *(les routes départementales)*:
D123, D124 etc

---

1 Read the information on pages 52 and 53 and do the quiz. Explain your answers.

  a Name three ways you could get from Britain to France.

  b Why are Joseph and Etienne Montgolfier famous?

  c Why might some people avoid motorways?

  d List 3 things a driver visiting France needs to remember.

2 List in French all the different ways to travel in the area where you live, using a dictionary to help you.

3 Choose a topic and write a short paragraph in English.

  a Write an article for your school magazine detailing the travel/transport records France holds.

  b Suggest some ways the French could reduce the number of deaths on the road.

  c Do you think it is a good idea to make motorists pay to use some motorways as they do in France?

With *la Carte 12-25*, young people get a 25% reduction on the price of train journeys.

French trains are run by a national rail company, the SNCF *(Société Nationale des Chemins de fer Français)*. Main lines all radiate out from Paris to major towns in the provinces and connect with the rail systems of neighbouring countries. Paris has six main stations, including the *Gare du Nord* (the Paris terminal for the Eurostar train from Britain).

You can buy a single *(un aller simple)*, a return *(un aller-retour)* or a variety of season tickets. Before you board your train, you have to punch *(composter)* your ticket in a machine – usually orange – at the entrance to the platform. If you forget, you risk getting a fine! French railways have the reputation of being efficient and punctual.

The star of the SNCF is the high-speed TGV *(train à grande vitesse)*. Reaching speeds of up to 515 km/hour, it is the fastest passenger train in the world. TGVs have aeroplane-style seating and advance seat reservations are obligatory. Because they run on special tracks, they only operate on certain main routes.

The first *métro* train: 5h30

The last *métro* train: 0h30

On most lines, there is a train every 5 minutes.

In Paris, the most convenient way to get around is by underground (*le métro*). *Métro* trains pass underneath the River Seine and many famous monuments such as the *Arc de Triomphe* and some lines come above ground. There are 16 lines and 297 stations (*stations de métro*, not *gares*!). *Métro* lines have numbers but are commonly named after the stop at the end of the line used to indicate the direction a train is running (eg *Direction Porte d'Orléans*). Many *métro* stations are named after famous people: the scientist Louis Pasteur, for example, or Bienvenüe who created the Paris *métro* in 1900.

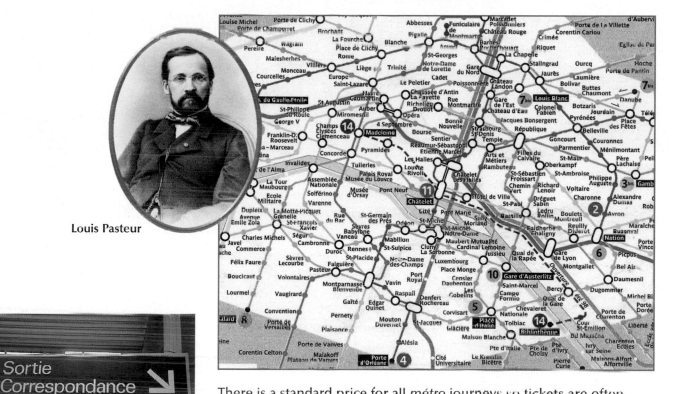

Louis Pasteur

If you need to change train look for the *correspondance* sign.

There is a standard price for all *métro* journeys so tickets are often bought in batches of 10 (*un carnet*) and kept to be used when needed. The same tickets can be used on buses as the RATP (*Régie Autonome des Transports Parisiens*) runs the buses as well as the *métro*. The RER (*le réseau express régional*) is an express *métro* serving the suburbs.

1 Read the information on pages 54 and 55 and do the quiz. Explain your answers.

   a At which Paris station do most British tourists arrive?

   b Do you buy tickets on board TGV trains?

   c How can you identify the different *métro* lines?

   d What is the RATP?

2 Using a dictionary, give the English equivalents of these signs found in a French station: *billeterie, sortie, quais, salle d'attente, horaires, guichets, consigne, renseignements.*

3 Choose a topic and write a short paragraph in English.

   a Write a paragraph about the *métro* for English-speaking tourists. Include details of times the trains run and any other useful information.

   b What are the advantages and disadvantages of having a single State-owned company running the railway network, as they do in France?

France's history

France has had many rulers over the centuries, among them: Clovis, the first king to be crowned in Reims cathedral in 496; the emperor Charlemagne, not very popular with French pupils for creating schools in the 9th century; Louis XIII, who established a very strong monarchy in the 17th century and the richest and most powerful of all, Louis XIV, the Sun King *(le Roi Soleil)*, who ruled from the grand palace of Versailles but left France bankrupt after his death.

In the late 18th century, a financial crisis brought about many social problems. The King, Louis XVI, and his wife, Marie-Antoinette, didn't really care about the people of France. At the same time, philosophers such as Diderot, Voltaire and Rousseau questioned the unfair principles of the monarchy. This led to the events known as the French Revolution *(la Révolution française)*.

On July 14th 1789, a Parisian mob, the *Sans-Culottes* ("without trousers", the name given to the Revolutionaries because of the style of trousers they wore), stormed the Bastille prison, a symbol of injustice. In August, an Assembly was set up. It produced the Declaration of the Rights of Man which embodied the principles of the Revolution and of the first Republic.

The next decade brought confusion and anarchy. Louis XVI and the Queen were guillotined in 1793, during *la Terreur*, the regime of Robespierre and his Committee of Public Safety, which sentenced scores of people to the guillotine. The Revolution had become a violent civil war. The French looked for strong leaders and found Napoleon Bonaparte.

Napoleon Bonaparte

In 1799, Bonaparte ended the Revolution by taking over. He crowned himself emperor in 1804. He was a brilliant politician: he established a powerful central administration and a strong code of law, still in effect today. His military genius and numerous campaigns almost gave him control of the entire European continent. After his defeat at Waterloo in 1815, he was exiled and replaced by a king, Louis XVIII.

Louis XVIII was eventually overthrown by Charles X. The people thought Charles X was too much of a dictator and they got rid of him during the July Revolution of 1830. The country then had an elected king, Louis Philippe, until 1848, when a nephew of Napoleon Bonaparte was elected president of the Second Republic before being proclaimed Emperor Napoleon III in 1852. When he lost the war against Prussia in 1871, he was ousted and replaced by a third Republic which lasted until 1940.

During World War II a very influential figure in French history emerged: *le Général de Gaulle*. He had organized the Resistance movement to free France of the German occupation and headed the government of the Fourth Republic in 1946. In 1958, he created the Fifth Republic, increasing the powers of the President. This is still in effect today.

Charles de Gaulle

Cette année, au collège, on étudie l'histoire de France du Moyen Âge jusqu'à la première guerre mondiale de 1914. C'est intéressant mais c'est compliqué!

Antoine, 14 ans

1 Read the information on pages 56 and 57 and do the quiz. Explain your answers.

a What was the regime in France before the Revolution?

b On what day was the first significant event of the Revolution?

c Who put an end to the Revolution?

d Who was General de Gaulle?

2 Read Antoine's bubble and translate it into English, using a dictionary to help you.

3 Choose a topic and write a short paragraph in English.

a Sum up the main reasons for the French Revolution in 1789.

b Do you think the use of the guillotine was justified during the Revolution? Argue for or against.

c Can you think of other examples in history where people have turned to strong but potentially overpowering leaders, like Napoleon?

The legacy of the Revolution

The French Revolution was a major event in the history of France and Europe. It abolished absolute monarchy and established equal liability to taxation. It began reforms in education and law. It shaped modern politics by defining key elements such as everyone's right to vote, human rights and civil equality.

Liberté, Égalité, Fraternité
The Revolution's ideals "Liberty, Equality, Fraternity," became the motto of liberal, democratic reforms in France and Europe in the 19th century. It is engraved, along with RF, *république française*, on most official buildings, like town halls.

Justice
Before the Revolution, justice wasn't very ... just! Only a judge could decide if someone was innocent or guilty. In 1791, the Assembly adopted a new system, still in use today: a jury of 12 citizens picked at random would debate with the judge before reaching a verdict.

La guillotine
The death penalty existed up to the 20th century. Executions varied according to the crime: some criminals were hanged, others burnt, some horribly tortured. In 1791, it was decided that death should be the same for all: beheading. According to some historians, between 30 000 and 40 000 people were guillotined during the French Revolution. The guillotine was used in France until the death penalty was abolished there, in 1981.

Did you know...?

The following were created during the French Revolution:

- The Constitution

- The French flag, *le Tricolore*

- The national anthem: *la Marseillaise*

- The symbol of the Republic: *Marianne*

- The division of France into *départements*

- Paper money: before 1789, there were only coins with the image of the king

- The metric system (*le système métrique*)

- The right to divorce

- Compulsory schooling for all children from 6 to 10

Incredible but true!

The Revolutionary government decreed that all citizens should eat the same bread: *le pain de l'égalité* (bread of equality). Napoleon 1st went further and regulated its size and weight! After 1945, bakers began making *la baguette*. Today, it is 80 cm long, weighs 250 grams and the price is still set by the State.

The French Revolution produced a document which was to have far-reaching consequences in the whole world: *La Déclaration des Droits de l'Homme et du Citoyen* (declaration of the rights of man and of the citizen).

La Déclaration des Droits de l'Homme et du Citoyen
● On 26th August 1789, the French Assembly produced 17 articles of universal importance. The first article read: *"Les hommes naissent et demeurent libres et égaux en droits."* (Men are born and remain free and equal in rights). This document set a precedent.
● On December 10th 1948, the United Nations adopted the Universal Declaration of Human Rights, reasserting the basic principles of the 1789 Declaration and adding new articles, e.g. equality between men and women, the right to asylum, to work, to education and culture, etc.
● On November 20th 1989, an international convention was signed in order to protect the rights of children. Only two countries did not sign: Somalia and the United States.

Some of the rights of young people in France today

Before 13	At 13	At 14	At 15	At 16	At 17	At 18 (majority)	At 23
Right to:	*Right to:*	*Right to*	*Right to*	*Right to:*	*Right to:*	*Right to*	*Right to:*
■ a surname, first name + nationality ■ an identity card ■ material and moral assistance ■ education (school compulsory from 6 to 16)	■ have a say about parents' divorce, custody arrangements and adoption ■ open a bank account (with parents' consent) ■ purchase common goods in shops	■ have a summer job ■ ride a moped (under 50 cc) ■ go into a bar without an adult (consuming non-alcoholic drinks only)	■ have sexual relationships with people over 15 ■ contraception ■ marry for girls (with parents' consent) ■ have own passport ■ see a doctor on one's own	■ leave school ■ work (max. 8 hours a day, no night shifts) ■ emancipation ■ ride a motorbike (under 125 cc) ■ learn how to drive, accompanied by an adult ■ go into a bar and drink wine, cider and beer	■ drive a motor boat with a licence	■ vote at elections ■ be a candidate in local elections ■ receive financial help from parents if still studying ■ hold a driving licence ■ be a blood or organ donor ■ travel abroad alone ■ drink any alcohol in a bar ■ marry for boys	■ be a candidate for the *Assemblée Nationale*, the European Parliament, the Presidency of the Republic.

1 Read the information on pages 58 and 59 and do the quiz. Explain your answers.

  a What does *RF* stand for on public buildings in France?

  b Until when was the guillotine used in France?

  c At what age can you get married in France?

  d Can you be an MP at 18?

2 Make a list in French of what you think are the six essential rights for someone your age, using a dictionary to help you.

e.g.

  1 **le droit d'***avoir une éducation.*

  2 **le droit d'***avoir un job*, etc.

3 Choose a topic and write a short paragraph in English.

  a Sum up the importance of the *Déclaration des Droits de l'Homme et du Citoyen*.

  b Look at young people's rights in France. How do they compare with your country?

France is like a giant jigsaw-puzzle: it is divided into nearly 36 800 pieces called *les communes*. This represents over half the local districts in the European community!

Communes are the basic unit of French administrative organisation. They vary from tiny villages (65% of *communes* have less than 500 inhabitants) to large towns (38 *communes* have over 100 000 inhabitants).

Each *commune* normally has a town hall *(une mairie)* and is run by local councillors *(les conseillers municipaux)*. They are elected every six years and they nominate the mayor *(le maire)*.

The town hall is where people have to register births *(les naissances)*, deaths *(les décès)*, marriages *(les mariages)* and divorces *(les divorces)* and where they get identity cards *(les cartes d'identité)*, passports *(les passeports)* and birth certificates *(les fiches d'état civil)*.

Mayors are important figures in local French life. They not only manage the affairs of the *commune* (budget, bye-laws, public order, etc.) but, as local representatives of the State, they or their deputy *(le maire-adjoint)* officiate at marriages.

Le Conseil Municipal Junior

Some *communes* have set up a young people's council: a number of 11-14 year-olds are elected by their fellow-pupils and meet up several times a year to discuss ideas for improving the quality of local life. They are given a budget to finance certain projets such as improving road safety or leisure facilities for young people.

Je suis membre du conseil municipal junior. Nous, on voudrait des classes d'informatique pour les enfants et les grands-parents à la médiathèque. C'est une bonne idée, non?

Olivier, 13 ans

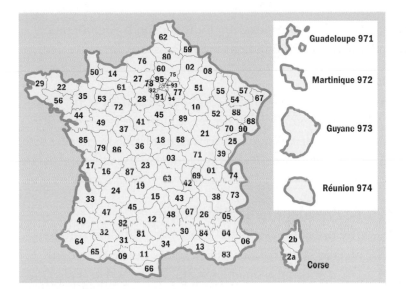

Several *communes* make up a *canton* and several *cantons* make up a *département*. There are 100 *départements*, 96 in mainland France and 4 overseas (*Martinique, Guadeloupe, Réunion* and *Guyane*). Most of them are named after a local river or mountain. They are run by a *préfet*, the representative of the State, and the *préfecture* is the "capital" town of the *département*, usually the largest or most central.

In 1960, the *départements* were grouped into regions. Mainland France has 22 *régions*, made up of 2 to 8 *départements*. Each of the four overseas *départements* is a region in itself. They are run by a *Conseil Général. Conseillers généraux* are elected every 6 years. In 1982, in an effort to decentralise power, a legislation gave *conseils généraux* greater autonomy: they have their own budget to run the economic, social and cultural life of the region.

Each region has a strong sense of its own identity, be it for historical, geographical or economic reasons. Some people in Corsica or the Basque country even feel their region should be independent. Corsica has a special status with an assembly with additional powers.

A road sign in the Basque country, in Basque as well as French

---

1 Read the information on pages 60 and 61 and do the quiz. Explain your answers.

  a What is the smallest administrative division called?

  b Who chooses the Mayor?

  c How many French *départements* are there?

  d What are the names of the four overseas *régions*?

2 Read Olivier's bubble. Using a dictionary, write down three things you'd ask for if you were a junior local councillor in your town. Start: *Je voudrais ....*

3 Choose a topic and write a short paragraph in English.

  a Sum up what the three tiers of local government are in France.

  b Do you think a *Conseil Municipal Junior* is a good idea? Why?

  c Research a French region and write a short paragraph summing up its main features.

The Presidents of the 5th Republic

Le Général Charles de Gaulle
1958-1969

Georges Pompidou
1969-1974

Valéry Giscard D'Estaing
1974-1981

François Mitterand
1981-1995

Jacques Chirac
1995-

French elections *(les élections)* are always on a Sunday. The ballot is secret and you must go to a booth *(un isoloir)* and close the curtain before placing the slip with the name of your chosen candidate in an envelope. When you place the envelope in the slot of the urn, a person reads out your name from the register and another shouts: *"A voté!"* (has voted). When no candidate has achieved an overall majority, there is a second round of the election *(le deuxième tour)* two weeks later.

France is a republic and the Government is chosen by democratic elections. All government buildings are in Paris.

Les citoyens français

Since 1848, French citizens have had the right to elect the people who are going to represent them through universal suffrage (everyone is entitled to vote). However, women had to wait until 1945 to be able to vote! To vote you must be over 18 and registered on the electoral list in your local town hall.

Le Président de la République

The president is elected every five years and can be re-elected several times. He appoints the Government and decides the main lines of its politics. He is also the Head of the Army. He never goes to the National Assembly but can send MPs messages. He can address the people through televised speeches and can consult them directly in a referendum. No woman has ever been elected president. The President lives and works in the *Palais de l'Élysée*.

Le Gouvernement

The President of the Republic appoints his Prime Minister, *le Premier ministre*, and approves his/her choice of ministers and secretaries of State (between 30 and 50).

The ministers meet the President every Wednesday morning for *le Conseil des ministres*. For the first time in 1991, a woman, Edith Cresson, was appointed Prime Minister. The Prime Minister's office is the *Hôtel Matignon*.

Le Parlement

The French parliament is made up of an Assembly and a Senate. They propose, discuss and vote on what will become law. They also control the Government's actions.

L'Assemblée nationale is made up of 577 members, *les Députés*, elected every five years. Less than 12.5% of MPs are women. If over half the *Députés* disapprove of its actions, they have the power to overthrow the Government. The Assembly sits in the *Palais Bourbon*.

Le Sénat is made up of 321 members, *les Sénateurs*, elected by the mayors and councillors for 9 years. Around 10% of Senators are women. The President of the Senate can replace the President of the Republic should he be unable to perform his duties. If there is a disagreement between the Senate and the Assembly, the *Députés* have the final say. Senators sit in the *Palais du Luxembourg*.

Political parties in France

French politics are characterised by a Left/Right division even if the border between the two is becoming blurred. There are over 20 parties in France and each one changes its name quite frequently.

The main right-wing party is the Republican *Union pour un Mouvement Populaire* which defeated the extreme right *Front National* in the presidential elections in 2002. The main left-wing parties are *le Parti Socialiste* and *le Parti Communiste*.

The ecologists appeared in 1974 and are divided into two rival factions: *Les Verts* (the Greens) and *Génération Écologie*, more right wing.

The most important group of the extreme left is *Lutte ouvrière* (Workers' Struggle) headed by a woman, Arlette Laguiller.

The French government

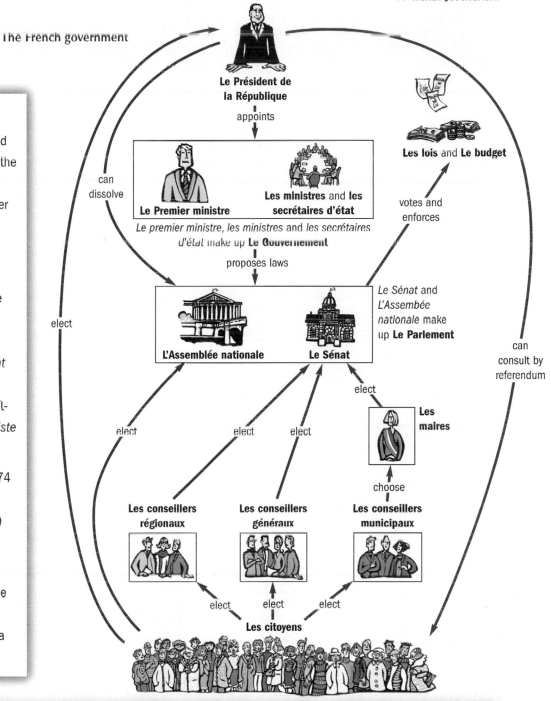

1 Read the information on pages 62 and 63 and do the quiz. Explain your answers.

  a What do you call someone who lives in a republic?

  b Is the French Prime Minister elected or appointed and by whom?

  c What is the residence of the President of the Republic?

  d Who decides what is to be law?

2 Draw up an organigramme of the British government and look up the French words in a dictionary.

eg. Parliament = *le parlement*

3 Choose a topic and write a short paragraph.

  a Sum up the position of women in the French political arena.

  b How does the French system of government compare with the British system? Write a paragraph summing up the main differences.

The French spend on average a total of 6 hours a day on the following:

- watching television (3 h 20 mins)
- listening to the radio (2 hours)
- reading newspapers (40 mns)

Television

Despite a recent increase in the number of channels available (more than 200), the French are watching slightly less TV than before, especially young people who spend more time playing video games and on the Internet. However, watching television *(regarder la télévision)* remains the favourite leisure activity in France and most national channels follow the same pattern which fits in with the French day. Morning programmes are between 7 and 9, with the lunchtime news at 1. Early evening entertainment programmes (games, series, etc.) start around 7 and are very popular. The evening news and weather start at 8, followed by the main primetime programme at 8:55. The content of the second part of the evening is more cultural (debates, current affairs, etc.). There are adverts on all national channels.

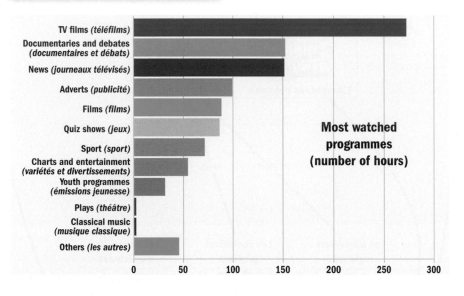

TV films *(téléfilms)*
Documentaries and debates *(documentaires et débats)*
News *(journeaux télévisés)*
Adverts *(publicité)*
Films *(films)*
Quiz shows *(jeux)*
Sport *(sport)*
Charts and entertainment *(variétés et divertissements)*
Youth programmes *(émissions jeunesse)*
Plays *(théâtre)*
Classical music *(musique classique)*
Others *(les autres)*

0   50   100   150   200   250   300

Most watched programmes (number of hours)

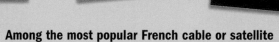

4 national public channels

- *France 2* (general interest)
- *France 3* (broadcasts national and regional programmes)
- *Arte* (Franco-German cultural channel)
- *France 5* (educational channel)

3 national private channels

- *TF1* (the oldest and most popular channel)
- *M6* (mainly music and series aimed at young people)
- *Canal Plus* (encoded pay-channel).

Among the most popular French cable or satellite stations

- *Canal J* (for 2 to 14-year-olds)
- *Canal Jimmy* (for fans of the 1960's and 1970's)
- *Planète* (documentaries)
- *Ciné Cinémas* (films)
- *Eurosport*
- *MCM* (music)
- *LCI (La Chaîne Info)* (continuous news)

Average number of radios in a home: 6

What type of radios do people have?

- a radio (*une radio*): 99%
- a radiocassette (*un radiocassette*): 86,2 %
- a radio alarm (*un radio-réveil*): 80,7%
- a car radio (*une autoradio*): 80%
- a tuner (*un tuner*): 77,7%
- a walkman with radio (*un baladeur*): 26,8%

La *Maison de la Radio* in Paris houses the national radio company *Radio-France* and its many different stations, none of which have commercial breaks (*France Inter, France Culture, France Musique, France Info* – the non-stop news station in Europe – etc.). You can attend free recordings and concerts here.

Radio

Listening to the radio (*écouter la radio*) is extremely popular in France, especially with young people. This is quite surprising given competition from more modern media. 99% of the French have at least one radio at home. 80% listen to the radio at least once a day: at home (64%), in the car (17%) and at work (16%).

In 1982, the French government allowed private radios (*les radios libres*) to broadcast. The choice of stations is now tremendous (more than 1800 stations). The main stations are *France Inter, RTL (Radio Télé Luxembourg)*, and *Europe 1* which offer a schedule of news, music, game shows, discussion programmes and magazine programmes.

> Ma station de radio préférée, c'est le Mouv'. La musique est super! J'écoute la radio le matin et quand je fais mes devoirs. Le soir, je regarde la télé, surtout les séries et les films.

Young people's favourite stations on FM offer mainly music: *Europe 2* (charts), *NRJ* (dance), *Sky Rock* (rap), *Fun Radio, Chérie FM*, etc. A national station called *Le Mouv'*, was created in 1997 in Toulouse for 15-24 year olds. It plays music (especially French rock) and has phone-ins but no commercial breaks.

Over 60% of young listeners always tune in to the same station. 67% wake up to the radio and 58% go to bed with the radio on.

---

1 Read the information on pages 64 and 65 and do the quiz. Explain your answers.

  a How many public TV channels are there in France?

  b Do the French watch more or less TV than before?

  c What radio station would you listen to for rap?

  d Who is the target audience of *le Mouv'* radio station?

2 Using a dictionary, list in French the types of TV programmes you like watching.

3 Choose a topic and write a short paragraph in English.

  a Sum up the differences and similarities between television in France and Britain.

  b What evidence is there that radio is not an outdated medium in France ?

  c Do you agree with having adverts on national channels as they do in France? Discuss the pros and cons of advertising on TV and radio.

The national dailies

(ranked according to sales)

L'Équipe (only sport)

Le Parisien/Aujourd'hui (popular press)

Le Monde (general interest)

Le Figaro (rightwing slant)

Libération (leftwing slant)

Les Échos (business and finance)

France Soir (tabloid)

La Tribune (business and finance)

L'Humanité (linked to the Communist Party)

Paris-Turf (horse racing)

La Croix (linked to the Church of France)

Some regional dailies

Ouest-France, Sud-Ouest, La Voix du Nord, Le Dauphiné Libéré, Nice-Matin, L'Est-Républicain, Les Dernières Nouvelles d'Alsace

Every year, the French government organises *La Semaine de la presse dans l'École* (Press in school week) when pupils learn about the various forms of media and how to use them critically.

Newspapers

French national daily newspapers are amongst the least bought and the most expensive in Europe. Less than 40% of the French read a national daily paper *(un quotidien national)*, compared to 85% in Britain. The number of different newspapers published has dropped from 26 to 11 since 1945, due to their cost and the advent of radio, television and other media.

The regional press is more successful than the national press, probably because it concentrates on local issues. *Ouest-France* is the top regional daily paper *(un quotidien régional)*. With a readership of over 20 million, it is second only to television.

There are newspapers specifically for children and teenagers: a daily paper for children aged 10 and over, *Mon Quotidien*, for example, and some weekly papers *(hebdomadaires)* like *Le Journal des Enfants*, *Les Clés de l'Actualité* and *Les Clés Junior*. They report national and international news and current affairs in a way that will appeal to young people.

You can buy a newspaper or a magazine at a newsagent's *(une maison de la presse)*, a newstand *(un kiosque à journaux)*, in supermarkets and wherever you see the sign *Presse*.

12-18 year-olds and the media

More than 50% use the Internet and 11% say they trust the information they find over the net.

51% say they trust television more than a newspaper or the radio.

93% think that it is essential to be aware of the news and current affairs

70% wish they could discuss current affairs and the media in class.

Magazines

The French are the biggest readers of magazines in the world. Every day, more than 67% of them read at least one magazine, mostly at home (86%), at friends' homes (7%), at work (4%) or in a waiting room (2%).

There are over 3 000 titles, including weekly (*hebdomadaire*), monthly (*mensuel*) and quarterly magazines (*trimestriel*). Titles disappear and hundreds of others start up every year. Every taste, interest and age group is catered for. Television magazines have the largest readership of them all (the most popular is *TV Magazine* with 14 million readers), followed by sports magazines (*L'Équipe Magazine* is the most popular of these). There are more than 80 titles for young people, from babies to students (*Okapi*, *Phosphore*). Women's magazines are quite popular (*Femme Actuelle* is 3rd in the top ten of weekly magazines). However, the most prestigious is probably *Elle*, which has about 30 foreign editions. The best-selling current affairs magazine is *Paris Match*, which blends highly illustrated news items with light features on celebrities (actors, royal families, etc.) from all over the world. Most national newspapers and magazines have an electronic version on the Internet.

---

1 Read the information on pages 66 and 67 and do the quiz. Explain your answers.

   a Do French people read more newspapers than magazines?

   b What is the best-selling newspaper in France?

   c What sort of magazine sells the most in France?

   d Would you buy *Paris Match* for an in-depth coverage of current affairs?

2 List magazines and newspapers in your country and write what they are in French, using a dictionary to help you,

e.g. *Kerrang – magazine hebdomadaire sur la musique*

3 Choose a topic and write a short paragraph in English.

   a Sum up the reasons given for the decrease in sales of French daily newspapers.

   b Children and young people are well catered for by the French press. How does that compare with Britain?

   c Look at what French 12–18 year-olds think of the treatment of the news in the media. Do you agree with them? Explain why.

Hit parade of summer jobs in France

1 in a hotel [un hôtel]

2 in sports activities [des animations sportives]

3 in a restaurant [un restaurant]

4 with firemen [les pompiers]

5 in a hospital [un hôpital]

6 in the transport sector [les transports]

Young people at work

Until fairly recently, the French school system did little to prepare pupils and students for the world of work. It now increasingly encourages visits to work places and work placements *(les stages en entreprises)*.

In France, teenagers are less likely to have a weekend job *(un petit boulot)* than in Britain: most go to school on Saturday mornings and tend to spend a considerable amount of time on their studies. No paper rounds for them!

The law stops teenagers under 14 having a job. 14 to 16 year-olds can have a summer job *(un job d'été)*, provided they have their parents' permission, and that they only perform light work for less than half of the holiday – no more than 35 hours a week, 7 hours a day with a 30-minute break every four and a half hours. They should earn at least 80% of the minimum wage *(le SMIC, around 7 euros an hour)* when they are 17, and at least 90% when they are 18.

To find a summer job, you need to look at or place small ads *(les petites annonces)*.

LONDRES : Hôtels, Restaurants et Pubs recherchent personnel pour jobs d'été. Postes pour débutants et pros. Jobs de serveurs, serveuses, hôtesses d'accueil, personnel de Fast Food et de Pub, barman etc. Âge minimum: 18 ans. Renseignements www.londonjob.net

CAMPING EN CORSE RECHERCHE ETUDIANT/E POUR POSTE DE RECEPTIONNISTE. SALAIRE 950 euros pour le mois. LOGE-NOURRI.

J'ai 15 ans et je recherche un petit boulot de ménage ou babysitting à Vannes pendant les vacances de Pâques. Appelez Sophie, 06 75 45 37.

J'ai 14 ans et j'ai un petit boulot: pendant les vacances et le week-end, je travaille dans le restaurant de mes parents: je suis serveuse!

Amandine

Jobs for the 21st century

- *fournisseur d'accès* (net provider)

- *administrateur web* (webmaster)

- *infographiste* (computer graphic artist)

- *netsurfeur* (net researcher)

Jobs for the future

In 1998, in order to curb unemployment *(le chômage)* (France has one of the highest unemployment rates in Europe at 9%), the government created and financed entirely new posts, *"les emplois jeunes"*. These aimed to help young people under 26 find employment while meeting the social needs of the local community: in education, health, culture, the environment, transport, etc.

A recent survey shows that work is very important to young French people and that they want a job which is exciting as well as financially rewarding. One of their chief worries is not being able to find a job when they finish school. Many young people are tempted by jobs in *une start-up*, a new and sometimes precarious business on the Internet. A job is no longer for life as it used to be a generation or two ago. Young people are often given fixed-term contracts (*CDD: contrat à durée déterminée*, not always renewable) and often work part-time or as temps. Work of this type has doubled in the last ten years and although it caters for more people, these jobs are not secure jobs.

Jobs are now less secure

1 Read the information on pages 68 and 69 and do the quiz. Explain your answers.

  a At what age can you have a summer job in France?

  b What is the most popular summer job?

  c Why do fewer French teenagers have weekend jobs than British teenagers?

  d What is *le SMIC*?

  e Are French teenagers worried by unemployment?

2 Look at the small ads on page 68. Which ad asks for waiters and waitresses? Do you need to be qualified? How old do you need to be? How much would you earn if you work as a receptionist at the Corsican campsite? What comes with the job? What does Sophie want to do?

3 Choose a topic and write a short paragraph in English.

  a What do you think are the main differences and similarities between French and British teenagers in relation to the world of work?

  b What types of *emplois jeunes* do you think could usefully be created in your local area?

1st May = *la Fête du Travail* (Labour Day)

The 1st May has been a bank holiday since 1947 (but workers don't get extra time off if it is on a Saturday or Sunday). Trade unions organise marches. The main rally is in Paris, between *Place de la Bastille* and *Place de la République* where speeches are made.

France has the lowest trade union membership rate in Europe (7% of workforce) yet the highest number of representative trade unions at national level.

- France's main employer is the State. A quarter of the labour force are civil servants.

- In 1973, France created *le SMIC (salaire minimum inter-professionnel de croissance)*. It affects 11% of wage earners and is the highest minimum wage in Europe at about 7 euros per hour.

- *L'ANPE (Agence nationale pour l'emploi)* helps the unemployed to find a job by providing ads and advice. With 9% of its population unemployed, France has one of the highest rates in Europe.

It's not all work!

One of the main changes in the working life of French people over the past 100 years has been the reduction in working hours by half.

A typical working day *(la journée de travail)* in France starts at around 9am. On average, the French spend 20 minutes travelling to work, which for over 70% is in the nearest town. Only 16% work in a different town and 4% work from home *(le télétravail)*. They don't finish work until 6pm-8pm but normally have a two-hour lunch break. Some shops and services (post offices, banks, etc) close at lunchtime and are normally closed one day during the week, often on Mondays, as well as on Sundays, although more people now work on Sundays (about a quarter of the working population).

French workers are legally entitled to 5 weeks holiday a year, which is more than in most countries. They also have 10 bank holidays *(les jours fériés)* and the possibility of getting extra days if they *faire le pont* (take a day off in order to bridge a bank holiday and a weekend).

In 2000, the legal working week for companies with 20 or more employees was 35 hours *(les 35 heures)* making it the shortest in Europe (the longest is in the UK). This was not always as successful as planned but left the French with more leisure time than they had ever had before.

In 1936, the left-wing government, *le Front Populaire*, gave workers their first paid holiday *(les congés payés)*: 2 weeks a year. In 1988, President Mitterrand's socialist government increased the entitlement to 5 weeks.

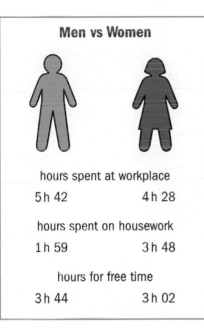

Men vs Women

hours spent at workplace

5 h 42   4 h 28

hours spent on housework

1 h 59   3 h 48

hours for free time

3 h 44   3 h 02

Another major change in French working life is that 80% of women aged between 25 and 55 now work (45% in 1968). They represent a growing part of the labour force (11.5 million out of a total of 26 million). Yet, despite legislation on equality at work, men with the same qualifications still obtain better-paid jobs (their salaries are 27.2% higher): women tend to do the least-skilled jobs, in sectors where salaries are lower. Employers still prefer taking on men. Unemployment amongst women is 3% higher than amongst men. While 40% of executives *(les cadres)* today are women, only 5% of these are heads of companies. The balance is likely to change slowly as there are now more girls than boys in higher education.

As in most other countries, the kinds of jobs people do *(les métiers)* have changed over the last hundred years. The proportion of workers in each of the three sectors, primary (agriculture, fishing, mining), secondary (industry and manufacturing) and tertiary (service industries) is the reverse of what it was in 1900. There are indeed fewer farmers *(les agriculteurs)*, fishermen *(les pêcheurs)* and miners *(les mineurs)* than ever before, fewer factory workers *(les ouvriers)*, shopkeepers *(les commerçants)* and craftsmen *(les artisans)* and far more white collar workers *(les cadres or les cols blancs)*. Another fast-growing sector which appeared in the late 1990s is the fourth sector *(le secteur quaternaire)*. It covers non-profit making organisations (social work, etc.) which employ nearly 2 million people, mostly part-time.

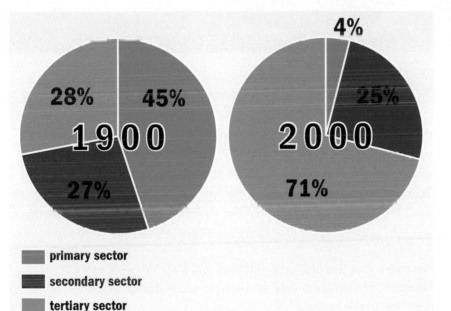

- ■ primary sector
- ■ secondary sector
- ■ tertiary sector

---

1 Read the information on pages 70 and 71 and do the quiz. Explain your answers.

  a Do French people tend to work far away from where they live?

  b Since when have the French been entitled to paid holidays?

  c What happens on May 1st?

  d What is *le SMIC*?

2 Make a list of jobs in French for each sector, as in the example. Look up more in a dictionary. *Primaire: un agriculteur/une agricultrice... Secondaire: un ouvrier/une ouvrière...*

Tertiaire: un professeur...

3 Choose a topic and write a short paragraph in English.

  a Sum up the main differences and similarities between a working day in France and in Britain.

  b What are the main changes affecting the working lives of the French over the last century?

  c Explain why French women tend to be paid less than men. How do you think the situation is likely to change?

France is a rich and powerful country – the 4th largest industrial power in the world.

In the 19th/20th centuries, traditional industries, particularly those in the North of France, such as the iron and steel industries and coal mining, helped France develop into the wealthy industrialised nation it is today. Many of these traditional industries have died out in recent years. This industrial decline has led to thousands of workers losing their jobs and to mines and factories being left derelict.

Nowadays, it is the hi-tech industries *(les industries de pointe)* – chemicals, pharmaceuticals, aerospace, etc. – that provide the jobs and bring in the money.

Every year, more than 3 million cars *(les voitures* or *les automobiles)* are constructed in France. About half of them are exported and sold abroad. A lot of the assembly work in the factories is done mechanically, by robots programmed by computer. Peugeot-Citroën is the largest car producer in France, in fact it is the 3rd largest in Europe (after the Italian firm Fiat and the German Audi/VW firm). One in ten French workers is employed in the motor industry.

France produced the TGV *(train à grande vitesse)*. This high-speed train runs at speeds averaging more than 200 km per hr. It is in service on several lines within France and also linking with major cities in neighbouring countries, such as Amsterdam and Brussels.

The Michelin rubber factory at Clermont-Ferrand is one of France's most important industries. It is famous for the tyres it makes, invented by the Michelin brothers in 1895. Its symbol of a man made from tyres is well-known in many countries. The factory is the biggest industry in the region employing more than 20 thousand people.

Au collège, j'aime beaucoup les sciences et la technologie. Je suis aussi fort en informatique. Plus tard, je voudrais étudier la chimie ou la technologie à l'université. Je voudrais être chercheur dans l'industrie chimique.

The *Ariane* rocket

Based in the south, in Toulouse, *Aérospatiale/Airbus Industrie* is the second most important aircraft manufacturer in the world. It is perhaps best known for creating – jointly with Britain – the Concorde supersonic jet, a great technological achievement, though less successful commercially. It produces not only Airbus planes, but also helicopters, space satellites and launchers, missiles and warheads. France started to develop the Ariane space programme in 1984. The Kourou rocket base, launchpad for several space rockets, is in Guyana in South America: although thousands of miles away from mainland France, Guyana is a French *département*.

France has developed computer technology and advanced communication systems. It has one of the most modern telecommunications systems in the world. It has made a name for itself creating and producing computer games *(les jeux électroniques)*, with PC games companies like Havas International and Ubi Soft.

The perfume capital

In the town of Grasse, there are more than 20 factories making perfume from flowers like roses, jasmine and orange blossom.

New technology has led to some workers losing their jobs, but it has also created new work opportunities (producing mobile phones *(les portables)*, DVD players *(les lecteurs de DVD*, etc.) that never existed in the past. It seems likely that in the future France will come to rely more and more on these new hi-tech industries.

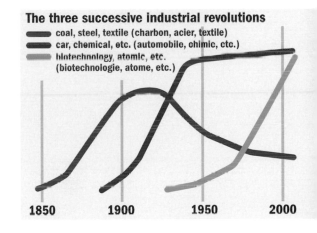

The three successive industrial revolutions
- coal, steel, textile (charbon, acier, textile)
- car, chemical, etc. (automobile, chimie, etc.)
- biotechnology, atomic, etc. (biotechnologie, atome, etc.)

1850   1900   1950   2000

1 Read the information on pages 72 and 73 and do the quiz. Explain your answers.

  a What were the 'traditional' French industries?

  b Is the French motor industry important?

  c What happens at Kourou?

  d What is *un portable*?

2 Translate into English the speech bubble at the top of the page. Use a dictionary to help if necessary.

3 Choose a topic and write a short paragraph in English.

  a Are transport-related industries important in France?

  b Use the Internet/the library to find out more about the French motor industry. Summarise what you learn.

  c Is modern technology a threat to jobs or an opportunity for new types of work?

France has more nuclear power stations than any other European country.

Since the 1970s the French government has been determined not to have to rely on imported energy, especially oil. France produces and uses different forms of energy.

The French have gone for nuclear power (*l'énergie nucléaire*) in a big way. More than three-quarters of the electricity consumed in France is produced by nuclear power (27% in UK). That is a higher proportion than in any other country in the world. They have more nuclear power stations than in any other European country – they produce more nuclear power than either Japan or Russia, only the United States produces more. In fact, France produces 50% of all nuclear power in the European Union. The largest nuclear reactor in the world is at Gravelines in the north of France. The uranium used in producing nuclear energy comes from the Limousin, Forez and Vendée regions of France.

Nuclear energy is a fairly cheap way of producing electricity, though it is not without its dangers. Some French people still protest about its use: 33% would like to see it scrapped completely, 48% would prefer not to open any new stations and only 14% would like to develop this form of energy. Only 55% are confident that using nuclear power is safe.

French scientists, inventors and researchers

1642 **the first calculator** (*machine à calculer*) invented by Blaise Pascal

1799 Philippe Lebon invented **gas lighting** (*l'éclairage au gaz*)

1826 **The first photograph** (*une photographie*) was an image fixed by Joseph Nicéphore Niépce

1829 Louis Braille invented **braille**, a special alphabet for the blind

1885 Louis Pasteur discovered a **vaccination** (*la vaccination*) for rabies and smallpox.

1895 Auguste and Louis Lumière invented **the cinema** (*le cinéma*)

1898 Marie Curie discovered **radium** (*le radium*). She won the Nobel Prize in 1903 and in 1911.

1934 Physicists Frédéric and Irène Joliot-Curie discovered **artificial radioactivity** (*la radioactivité artificielle*)

1972 Mathematician René Thom proposed the **chaos theory** (*la théorie des catastrophes*)

1983 Luc Montagnier discovered the **Aids virus** (*le virus du sida*)

France also produces other forms of energy. The world's only tidal power station (*centrale d'énergie marémotrice*) is on the Rance estuary in Brittany. As the tide goes out, it turns machines that produce electricity. Hydro-electric power is quite common in the Alps where cheap, clean electricity can be produced by damming steep fast-flowing streams. Solar energy (*l'énergie solaire*) is also used to a limited extent: there are stations in Corsica and in the Pyrenees.

Since 1969, France has been creating technological new towns called *technopoles*. They group together educational establishments, businesses and research laboratories, allowing scientific researchers and industrialists to work in close proximity. The first *technopole* created was Sophia-Antipolis, near Nice, in the south of France.

It remains to be seen whether French scientists will be able to find solutions for some of the nation's main concerns:

● global warming (*le réchauffement climatique*) which could bring about the rise in sea levels

● the hole in the ozone layer (*le trou dans la couche d'ozone*) which is reducing protection from the harmful damage done by the rays of the sun

● chemical industrial pollution (*la pollution chimique produite par l'industrie*) which contaminates water, the earth and the air

● acid rain (*les pluies acides*) which is caused by air pollution from factories, traffic, heating, etc.

There is a current shortage of scientific researchers but France has always been an inventive nation and will undoubtedly make great scientific and technological contributions to the world for years to come.

---

1 Read the information on pages 74 and 75 and do the quiz. Explain your answers.

　a What is the most popular form of energy in France?

　b Are most French people in favour of nuclear energy?

　c What is the French for 'global warming'?

　d Why are the Lumière brothers famous?

2 Use the Internet/library to find out about British inventions.

Use a dictionary to help you make a list of them in French.

3 Choose a topic and write a short paragraph in English.

　a Advantages and disadvantages of France relying heavily on nuclear power.

　b Are *technopoles* a good idea?

　c Use the Internet/library to find out more about a French scientist or inventor and summarise what you learn.

New Caledonia
(Nouvelle-Calédonie)

Vietnam
(Viêt-nam)

Laos
(Laos)

Cambodia
(Cambodge)

Mauritius (Île Maurice)
Reunion (Réurion)

Madagascar
(Madagascar)

Switzerland
(Suisse)

Luxembourg
(Luxembourg)

Tunisia
(Tunisie)

Algeria
(Algérie)

Ivory Coast
(Côte d'Ivoire)

Belgium
(Belgique)

France
(France)

Morocco
(Maroc)

Senegal
(Sénégal)

Guinea
(Guinée)

French Guyana
(Guyane)

Martinique
(Martinique)

Louisiana
(Louisiane)

Guadeloupe
(Guadeloupe)

Quebec
(Québec)

77

Useful French websites

ados.fr
A site for teenagers
www.ados.fr/

aéroports de Paris
The official website for Parisian airports, containing maps, timetables, and general information
www.adp.fr

annonces-carrieres.com
A French job search website
www.annonces-carrieres.com

campingfrance.com
An interactive website containing information about campsites all over France
www.campingfrance.com

l'escale.net
Everything you need to know about special celebrations in France
www.lescale.net/fetes.html

l'etudiant.fr
The online version of the student-orientated magazine
www.letudiant.fr

fff.fr
The official website for the French football team
www.fff.fr

france 3
State-run television network on the web, with tons of information and daily news.
www.france3.fr

greenpeace.fr
Information about the French division of Greenpeace
www.greenpeace.fr

guadeloupe.fr
Tourist information on Guadeloupe
www.guadeloupe-fr.com

Martinique
Information on Martinique
www.touristmartinique.com

meteo.fr
The online weather forecast for France
www.meteo.fr/meteonet

mont-saint-michel.net
A website containing information about and pictures of Mont St. Michel and other tourist attractions in Brittany
www.mont-saint-michel.net

Montivilliers cinema
A virtual guide around a French cinema, with information about films currently showing in France and those coming soon
www.infoceane.com/gaumont/index2.html

M6Music
Music site
www.m6music.fr

Nomade, Yahoo, Google
French search engines
www.nomade.fr
www.yahoo.fr
www.google.fr

parisvisite.fr
An online guide to Paris
www.parisvisite.tm.fr

laposte.fr
The French postoffice's official website
www.laposte.fr

quebecweb.com
A comprehensive online guide to Quebec
www.quebecweb.com/introfranc.html

Restaurant Berthoud
A Parisian restaurant's website, including menus and photos
www.resto.fr/berthoud/home-fr.htm

SEVE
Information about this environmental group and the work it does in Nantes
www.seve.nantes.fr

tele7jours.com
The online version of a French TV magazine
www.tele7jours.com

Index